W9-BRF-835

BRANDON,

I HOPE THIS HELPS YOU

FOCUS, PRIORITIZE AND

GET IN THE "ONE - DAY

CONTRACT" MENTALITY AS

MUCH AS IT DID FOR

ME.   ENJOY ⌐

Durhon

THE ONE-DAY
CONTRACT

THE ONE-DAY
CONTRACT

How to Add Value to Every Minute of Your Life

Rick Pitino

with

Eric Crawford

ST. MARTIN'S PRESS ❧ NEW YORK

THE ONE-DAY CONTRACT. Copyright © 2013 by Rick Pitino and Eric Crawford. All rights reserved. Printed in the United States of America. For information, address St. Martin's Press, 175 Fifth Avenue, New York, N.Y. 10010.

www.stmartins.com

The Library of Congress Cataloging-in-Publication Data is available upon request.

ISBN 978-1-250-04106-7 (hardcover)
ISBN 978-1-4668-3721-8 (e-book)

St. Martin's Press books may be purchased for educational, business, or promotional use. For information on bulk purchases, please contact Macmillan Corporate and Premium Sales Department at 1-800-221-7945, extension 5442, or write specialmarkets@macmillan.com.

First Edition: October 2013

10 9 8 7 6 5 4 3 2 1

To my five children, Michael, Chris, Richard, Ryan, and Jaclyn—the one fist that always stays together. To my wife, Joanne, whose laughter has always taught me the meaning of a good life.

—Rick Pitino

To my mother, Jackie Crawford, and my grandmother, Lucille Crawford—women who fought off cancer with toughness and grace.

—Eric Crawford

CONTENTS

THE ONE-DAY
CONTRACT

INTRODUCTION

Best. Week. Ever.

Those were the three words I kept hearing, on television and during interviews, as well as from fans and friends, even before our University of Louisville basketball team beat Michigan for the NCAA Championship. It's true, I had an amazing week. Our team made it to the Final Four, and while I was learning via phone call that I'd been elected to the Naismith Memorial Basketball Hall of Fame, my son Richard called to tell me he had been hired at Minnesota, becoming the youngest head coach in the Big Ten Conference. On top of all that, a horse in which I was part owner won the Santa Anita Derby to punch his ticket for the Kentucky Derby.

People were marveling at my good fortune. And I'll be honest—I was marveling at my good fortune. A lifetime's worth of blessing, it seemed, was bestowed during one wondrous week. I was incredibly grateful, and it was more than I deserved. After we won the championship game, I was asked repeatedly to reflect on the preceding week, and what it had been like to have the "best week ever."

Looking back on all of it, the things everyone was talking about were not, in themselves, what truly made it great. In fact, it wasn't so long ago that the media was reporting I'd had the "worst week ever." What happened between the worst of times and what wound up as the best of times—and what made our championship run possible in the first place—gets at the heart of this book.

This book is unlike any other I have undertaken. I began writing it the summer before our championship season, and was piecing it together in my mind long before that. While others have been focused on career, basketball, and success, this book began with just one goal. Plain and simple, it began as an instrument to help people through the most difficult times of their lives. There's no question we live in trying days, just look at a newspaper or watch the nightly news. But most of us don't have to do that. We can see the evidence in our own lives. We all know about tough times. In this book, I will talk to you about mine.

A remarkable thing happened while this book was

being put together. As I was writing about overcoming adversity, the power of focus, dealing with doubt, the importance of humility, prospering through pressure and the other ideas here, my team was putting each of those principles on display. The special young men I was coaching were putting into practice many of the precepts I will share in this book. They, in essence, wrote the conclusion, provided the happy ending. They proved that these principles work.

They are fundamentals that are badly needed today, by all of us. A basketball season on the mountaintop for me does not change the fact that for many people these remain the most challenging, even desperate, of times. And the memory of adversity is never far away in my own life.

We live in an age warped by worry. Whether through foreclosure, stock market difficulties, or downturns in the housing or job markets, people who never thought they would have to deal with the crushing weight of financial uncertainty have found themselves facing that very problem. Bankruptcies are widespread. Others take retirement, and then find themselves struggling to live off the interest of their savings. Many reaching retirement age aren't sure whether they should stop working. Conservative investments are no longer reliable sources of income. Guarantees are gone. So many people of all ages in many walks of life feel there is nowhere to turn.

A 2011 survey by the American Psychological Association listed money as the No. 1 cause of stress in the United States, with the economy at No. 3 and housing costs at No. 7. Economic changes have many worried about the stability of their situation.

We live in a time troubled by tragedy—the Sandy Hook shootings, the Boston Marathon bombing. Places never before associated with violence now exist under a shadow that affects us all. Random violence is on the rise. When terrorists attacked the United States on September 11, 2001, something changed in our national psyche. A sense of security was shattered. For those of us who suffered personal losses that day, life has never been the same, and the ramifications will last forever. My whole perspective on life changed after 9/11 and the death of my brother-in-law, Billy Minardi. I've said it many times: Our life as a family, and particularly my wife and I, will never be the same. It has affected us like nothing else. It has changed the way we think, the way we view the past and the future. Even for those who haven't lost people close to them, such senseless acts take a toll.

We are a society sapped by stress. We sleep too little and eat too much. Every day you see it—people are on edge, angry and frustrated, or depressed and even hopeless. Most of us have an idea how to handle adversity. But stress is a different matter. It is like a poisonous pill that you take in a daily dose. As the stress of life has increased, we have become an increasingly overweight and unhealthy nation. We must immediately focus on stress relief so we don't suffer its debilitating side effects. Health and health care have become major sources of worry, and one of the most heated subjects of our national debates.

And above all else—because of everything we are facing—we are distracted. Our children cannot pay attention. Our adults are looking for escape.

All of these things will sap you of your energy, rob you of your resilience, and distract you from the focus that can be the lifeline that pulls you through the difficulties and back onto the road to your goals. So many times, whether in public life or on a smaller scale, I have seen people struggle when circumstances have overtaken them. I have experienced it in my own life.

This is not a book about how to avoid difficult times, though many of the chapters here may help you do just that. Instead, this is a book about what to do in the midst of the storm. What to do when the mistakes have been made, when you face the full-court press, when the bills pile up, the job interviews don't come, the investments tank, or the public embarrassment strikes. It is a book about keeping life together when it seems to be falling apart, whatever the reason, and emerging victorious on the other side.

My goal in writing this book is to share some of my experience in these areas. When I wrote *Success Is a Choice* in 1998, I received more than a thousand letters from people saying the book had made a difference in their lives. That book was about overachieving. This book is about overcoming. It is a message that is needed today in many areas of life by a wide range of people.

I have been through periods of great personal grief, professional and personal failure and frustration, as well as great prosperity and career accomplishment. At the University of Louisville, I've faced adversity from outside circumstance and of my own making, and I've experienced the rewards of strong friendships and great success.

As you embark on these pages, consider that the idea for this book was born out of some very difficult experiences, but by the time the project was completed, everyone was saying I'd experienced the "best week ever." There is hope, and help, in these difficult times. Sometimes, in fact, the strength we must gather to get through the hard times is what drives us up the mountain.

One problem today is that the obstacles seem so overwhelming that we can't realistically see the better future that could be ours. That's why I'm sharing my own method, a tool I used to get through some of my most difficult times, and one I have used for the past several years. Essentially, I have kept myself on a one-day contract, every single day. I will explain to you what that means, and why it works, throughout the following pages.

Being honored by the Hall of Fame and standing on the NCAA victory platform watching the "One Shining Moment" video were experiences to treasure. There is truth to all of the media's "best week ever" statements.

But one of the greatest moments was not amid the falling confetti and cutting nets. When Kevin Ware went down with a broken leg in the regional final against Duke, it was a terrible thing, probably the most painful sports injury I'd ever personally witnessed. But what grew out of it was something beautiful: the way his teammates responded with genuine, unabashed concern and love; the way our captain, Luke Hancock, knelt by his side to pray; the way our trainer, Fred Hina, rushed to him, covered the exposed leg bone with a towel, and went about stabilizing him; the way our equipment manager, Vinny Tatum, and strength coach, Ray Ganong, also rushed to comfort him; and finally, the way Kevin himself found the presence of mind and strength of character in that moment to think not of himself but of the rest of us, to urge us to win the game. Very seldom in life do you see such a profound response to adversity on such a public stage. The courage, love, and toughness embodied in all that were unforgettable. And when

I walked into Kevin's hospital room and the doctors told me he was going to be fine, that was one of the greatest moments. His ability to overcome adversity, to tell all of us, "I'm going to be fine, just win the game," and the spontaneous emotion and the strength of our players to persevere, were together the biggest victory. The one message I gave our team last year as well as this year was that you can go 31–2, but right or wrong, you will be judged on the final exam, how you play in the postseason. The regular season is just jockeying for NCAA Tournament position. The interesting thing about our championship team is that Kevin Ware wound up being the inspirational leader and Chane Behanan the physical presence. But both players were suspended during parts of the regular season. After their suspensions, I sat them down and told them, nobody will remember a day of this if you'll go out and have a successful finish. And boy, was that the case for them!

At the beginning of the 2013 postseason, Adidas sent our team warm-up shirts that said, "Rise to the Occasion." Watching Kevin and our team rise to that difficult occasion and grow from it turned one of my worst moments on a basketball court to the best week ever.

This book is about that journey, not just within a basketball season, but within life.

No matter what your situation as you open this book, nor my situation while writing it, we are faced with the responsibility of moving forward. We owe it to our families, our communities, and ourselves. No matter how difficult and distracting life is, our job is to focus, to work through it, to keep our eyes and our efforts where they belong. Every day, you can find stories about people who could not do that, whose lives or careers left the tracks. We know what stresses people. We have to come up with solutions. People are suffering. But adversity does not mean that you cannot experience victory— far from it. I am proof of that, and so are many others you will meet in these pages. If this book in some small way can ease the pain or help spark the climb by sharing the life lessons from thirty-five years of coaching, then the pages that follow will have accomplished their goal.

1

It Begins with Humility

More than any play I drew up on the board in our locker room, more than any strategy or concept we used during our national championship season, one word paved the way for everything that would follow: humility.

This probably is not the way most books following a national championship begin. There are victories to talk about, stories to tell, and lessons to learn. Humility is not even a basketball word. You might ask, where does this guy, or any basketball coach, get off talking about humility? I agree that humility is scarce in the athletic world. Egos run rampant, as much on the sidelines as on the court. The egotistical coach, the arrogant athlete, they are stereotypes that too often ring true.

Here at the outset of this book, you should understand that there are two ways to handle subjects as a coach or teacher. You can teach people or try to help them from showing them how you succeeded, or you can allow them to see and learn from your failures. The former is much more fun. But the latter often is more instructive. In this book, I not only will talk about successes and how they came about, but failures, too, in the hope that both sides will be helpful for some; because we all come up short at some point.

I was not a picture of humility for much of my career. That is one reason I want to talk about it first. The other reason is this: Without humility, no other principle or lesson I talk about in this book will hit home. It is the key to everything that follows.

When our players came back to campus before school started for the 2012–13 season, I knew there was a great danger of becoming complacent or resting on the success of having made the Final Four the previous April. When we got the team together, the theme of my first discussion in our first meeting was humility. It was the theme of my first speech to our fan base during our annual Tipoff Luncheon in October. And it was the last word I wrote on the board after every victory through our entire season, right through the NCAA championship game. For our team, humility was the key to staying focused and to keeping a winning mind-set, as well as the key to accepting setbacks and turning them to positives. Most of our players embraced the lesson of humility, which is a remarkable thing for a group of young people.

It was more than the key for our players. It was the key for me. The longer I live and the more I experience, the more I believe that humility is the quality essential to sustained success, and a lack of it is the major stumbling block for those who find success for a time, then lose it. I'm not claiming to have perfected the trait, but I have learned its importance, and am learning to let it take root in my life and work. The lesson of humility comes to everyone eventually. Either you learn its value, or life drills it into you—and life can be a painful teacher. It is a lesson best learned before life makes you another case study. Let me give you an example: myself.

We all have our share of personal regrets. My greatest professional regret might surprise you. It wasn't leaving the University of Kentucky and walking into my first professional failure with the Boston Celtics. Failure is not final, and I always have said it is fertilizer for future success. No, my great regret from a professional standpoint is that I was not humbler at an earlier age. Here is how it worked for me. My early coaching career was a succession of surprising rebuilding jobs, each more celebrated than the one before. My first head coaching job was at Boston University. The team had won seventeen games combined in the two years before I arrived and hadn't had a winning season in fifteen years. Within five years we had made the NCAA Tournament. After working as an assistant coach to Hubie Brown for the New York Knicks, I took over as head coach at Providence College, which had just finished a 12–20 season. In my second season, we went to a Final Four. The next season I had a dream job, head coach of the New York Knicks. For a kid who grew up just eight blocks from Madison Square Garden, at 26th Street, it was as much as I could ask for. They'd won just twenty-four games the year before. In my second season, we won the franchise's first Eastern Division championship in nearly two decades.

From there it was on to the Roman Empire of college basketball, the University of Kentucky. We took a program famously crippled by NCAA probation and were back in the Final Four in four years, and won a national title in six. Professionally, everything I touched seemed to be turning into gold.

Over the course of that time, I developed a feeling that much of that success was about me and what I was doing. It was difficult not to feel that way. There's no question when you coach at Kentucky, you fall into a trap of thinking you're much better than you really are, because of the adulation and attention. It is constant and seems to come in a never-ending supply. I did not know it in the midst of it, but that arrogance, that thinking of yourself as the best, is one of the biggest reasons successful people stumble and fail. It helped lead me into an error, but it was a fortunate one.

I was very lucky to have left that atmosphere when I did. I look back at my time at Kentucky and realize I didn't carry myself with the humility necessary to foster more lasting relationships. Thankfully, I was able to build some with several remarkable people, anyway, that remain to this day. Because I left when I did, after being on top for some great years, I had a good ending. Most Kentucky coaches have not. Adolph Rupp didn't; he was in a fierce battle to keep coaching. Joe B. Hall retired under fire despite winning a national title and reaching three Final Fours. Eddie Sutton left in turmoil. Tubby Smith never got his just credit for the outstanding job he did. His major problem was winning the championship too soon. So for me, leaving Kentucky personally wasn't a bad thing. I recognized that I was falling into a trap with all that adulation; but I really didn't understand completely the consequences until I failed with the Celtics. If I hadn't left, I might not have learned that important lesson of humility. Instead, the experience taught me a great deal and I emerged from my time in Boston with the knowledge that I needed to live my life more humbly. I retained that knowledge, but from time to time I would forget it, or not put it into practice, much to my dismay and detriment, which I will discuss during this book.

The consequences of not learning humility can be tragic. If we don't always see these consequences in our own lives, we should be able to recognize them all around us. Not learning humility is, for one thing, an expensive lesson. In 2009, *Sports Illustrated* estimated that 60 percent of NBA players are broke within five years after their playing careers are over, and 78 percent of NFL players are facing serious financial distress just two years after their retirement. Others might tell you it's a lack of discipline or poor financial advice that brings this about. I'm convinced that more than anything else, in most of these cases, it's a deficit of humility.

Look at the headlines to see examples of people with great talent who fail in many ways. What usually isn't in the headlines or the stories is the root cause of their failure. People could see it coming for Terrell Owens, the onetime dominant receiver of the National Football League, the player who at the top of his game once said, "I love me some me!" Here was a guy who once caught a touchdown pass over two defenders, grabbed a marker from someone behind the end zone, autographed a ball, and then tossed it to one of his financial advisors. The flamboyant celebrations, the constant need to be in the spotlight even off the field, the brash pronouncements, these are typical of the kind of arrogance displayed in all areas of life today, even if Owens is an extreme example. As high as he was riding—and he made $80 million from 2000 to 2010—Owens took wild financial risks. He made questionable real estate deals. He lost $2 million in an electronic bingo venture in Alabama, an investment that not only was made on an illegal enterprise, but in violation of NFL gambling rules. In 2011, with his football performance sliding, he went to a judge in Georgia asking the court to reduce his support payments to the four mothers of his four children. His Georgia home was in foreclosure. In January of 2012, he told *GQ* magazine that to anyone who texts him asking him where he is, he responds with a three-word message, "I'm in hell." Yet he still was not heeding life's call to humility.

This is a story that is repeated with painful regularity. The mistakes Owens made, while on a much larger scale, perhaps, are mistakes that many make. NFL player Adam "Pacman" Jones recently told a gathering of incoming league rookies that he once blew a million dollars in a single weekend. Beside him on the stage, Owens remarked, "Man, you crazy." And if Terrell Owens calls you crazy, you can take it to the bank. Self-aggrandizement, alienation of friends, family, or teammates, a tragic tendency to overestimate one's talent that leads to overreaching, they all are traits of people who lack humility.

This also is a story that is not new. The ancient Greeks had a word for this very situation: hubris. It means extreme confidence or arrogance to the point that one loses touch with reality and overestimates one's abilities. Often in Greek mythology and drama, their heroes would have great success, only to demonstrate hubris, bite off more than they could chew, and be laid low. The Greeks took this concept so seriously that hubris was a crime in ancient Athens. To humiliate a defeated foe was a crime.

Today, it is commonplace. NFL receivers aren't the only ones who fall into the trap. Some of the most insecure people are movie stars. To see the Mel Gibsons of the world achieve such stunning success, believe they cannot fail, and then be brought low out of arrogance and lack of humility is becoming a frequent narrative. Nowhere is it more personified than in Charlie Sheen. His reckless behavior, combined with a complete refusal to honestly assess himself, led him to assert that he was "winning" even as he was losing stature and face in the entertainment world, not to mention the leading role on a top-rated television show he had helped build. That he capitalized on his runaway arrogance with a so-called comedy tour shouldn't obscure the truth. What he achieved was not true success, but mere notoriety, and not even the best kind. By failing to embrace humility and clinging in desperation to his own arrogance and misplaced belief in himself, Sheen continued the cycle of self-destruction that was leading to his problems. The same cycle can be seen in many fields, from business leaders who saw no limits to their income or luxuries, to politicians who thought they were on a roll that could not be stopped, only to be run out of office. The list of those for whom humility not only might have saved a fortune, but their future, is long and star-studded.

I can see how it worked in my life. Whether it was Boston University, the Knicks, Providence, or Kentucky, every downtrodden program I took over turned around dramatically. So when I looked at the situation with the Boston Celtics, who were to get two of the top six picks in the upcoming NBA Draft Lottery, why would it be any different? Because I lacked humility, I just couldn't accept the possibility that I had only a 28 percent chance of getting the best-case scenario, the No. 1 and No. 2 picks. Of course I would get those picks, I reasoned. If I had been humbler, if I had been more aware of where my success came from, I would have looked at that situation and understood that the team was over the salary cap, that the odds were against getting Tim Duncan, the best player in that year's draft, and that it was not the great opportunity I was making it out to be. I might still have gone to the NBA, but it would have been a different job, had I understood better why you win. A lack of humility clouded my judgment.

Lacking humility makes you overextend. It makes

you feel immune not only from common consequences, but sometimes the law. Mike Tyson spent time in jail, and then lost his considerable fortune because of a ridiculous lifestyle of consumption and surrounding himself with bad advisors. People who lack humility often do this. Rather than surround themselves with more talented people with whom they would have to share credit and success, they pick the wrong people, and rarely share the credit. Show me a chief executive officer who keeps all of a $20 million bonus instead of passing some of it along to his fellow executives, and I'll show you someone who lacks humility, and is heading for a fall. Humility forces you to treat people around you better, to share with people, to carry them with you in any success you have. Humble people do that. That's why you see people like John Wooden, maybe the greatest coach of all time in any sport, or Mike Krzyzewski, who is the modern-day John Wooden, sustain success for so long. You can readily see their humility. That doesn't mean they don't have flaws, don't get angry or make mistakes. Everybody does. But the key that opens up all the greatness is humility.

Read this list of athletes who have filed for bankruptcy, and consider the cost of not learning this valuable lesson: Warren Sapp, Dennis Rodman, Allen Iverson, Mike Tyson, Marion Jones, Lawrence Taylor, Antoine Walker, Latrell Sprewell, Evander Holyfield,

Michael Vick, Travis Henry, Lenny Dykstra, Kenny Anderson, and Leon Spinks. And that list is far from complete.

Even for those whom it doesn't ruin financially, a lack of humility can bring other difficulties. In every player I have coached who has not reached his potential on and off the court, the common missing element in his life and attitude is humility. The overspending, buying ten watches, the decadent lifestyle, the entourages, the unrealistic expectation of their own stature and longevity—all this leads to poor choices and reckless decision making. There are many athletes who believe that because they are invincible at times on the court, it will spill over into other areas. This is a crucial misjudgment, and it all stems from a lack of humility. So many athletes I've coached are struggling right now. Every day, I hope they will find humility and become more like Jamal Mashburn, who was the opposite. He never thought he was good enough, and worked every day to get better. He wasn't a so-called McDonald's All-American, and he felt hard work and a willingness to listen to every suggestion for improvement were his road map to success. Jamal seemed to have a blueprint for how humility works in athletics. He was one of the most popular and respected players in University of Kentucky history. People sensed his humble spirit and were drawn to him. Jamal knew how to save and

21

develop a lifestyle that was healthy and humble for his family. He also invested wisely for his future. Today he is the CEO of a Lexus/Toyota dealership and currently owns pieces of franchises with Papa John's, Outback Steakhouse, and Dunkin' Donuts, and no one outside his inner circle would even know it. I only wish Jamal would serve as an example for all my players, not only in how to act, but how to develop a successful life down the road.

A lack of humility can damage your influence on others. As I watched New York Jets coach Rex Ryan go about his brash predictions, including guaranteeing a victory in the 2012 AFC Championship game, it just blew me away—and I'm from New York! I was confused about why he was doing this. Confidence is instilled in private meetings as well as in the locker room, with just you and your team, your own family hearing what you think of their skills and abilities to win—that sacred locker room, which has been pried open to the public more and more with each year of advancing technology. He had everything to lose and very little to gain. Everyone in the business tells me he's an outstanding football coach. I'm hoping the lesson he learned in 2012 brings about true success for him and his organization.

I'm also confused as to why Tim Tebow is such a lightning rod, why his spiritual belief rubs so many the wrong way. Is it because it is so out in the open? Or is it because people's own spiritual inadequacies or insecurity about faith move them to anger when someone else displays it openly? Tebow deflects all accomplishment toward others and God. Who does that hurt? It can't hurt anyone. Perhaps people don't think his faith is real, that it's an act. But if it's an act, he's one of the greatest actors since Spencer Tracy. He may not be the best quarterback, but he's a humble, hardworking young man who has accomplished so much in his life because he truly understands humility and typifies the proverb, "A man's pride will bring him low, but a humble spirit will obtain honor."

Maybe his coach for a while in New York, Rex Ryan, learned some of those lessons. After the 2012–13 season, he told reporters that he thinks his bravado might have hurt his team, and that he plans to tone it down.

"I've got to look at the entire dynamic of what I say, and how it doesn't just affect me," he said.

That recognition is the beginning of a humble mindset. On an even grander scale, LeBron James suffered the consequences of arrogance in the realm of personal popularity. James is not a bad person, and should be genuinely well liked around the league. But he staged a terribly conceived production when he decided to leave the Cleveland Cavaliers for the Miami Heat. "The Decision," a one-hour television show to extol his greatness while announcing his new NBA home, with a hastily tacked-on charity element after the initial negative reaction, brought him nothing but derision from basketball fans around the country. When the Heat lost in the NBA Finals in his first season, they did so to the delight of most basketball fans. James did not respond well even then, intimating that fans who criticized him would go back to their dreary lives while he would keep living in wealth. His jersey sales slipped from No. 1 in the league to No. 4. A year later in the NBA Finals, however, James performed brilliantly, like the most talented player in the league that he is. When asked after winning the title what enabled him to rise to the occasion, he said, "Losing in the Finals last year. It humbled me." James found his way back when he found humility. He then said the right things, began playing for the right reasons, was able to let go of the bitterness he felt over the criticism he'd taken and look at himself in an accurate light. A year later, LeBron James cemented his place as the game's best player by leading the Heat to a second straight championship.

By contrast, Kevin Durant of the Oklahoma City Thunder is beloved in the basketball world, even though his team lost to James and the Heat in the Finals. Why? Durant plays the game humbly and does not seek to draw all the attention to himself. His style of play is refreshing. Durant is old-school. He's one of only a handful of players who will speak with the media before games as well as in postgame sessions. Before last season, he ranked LeBron James and Kobe Bryant as No. 1A and 1B in the NBA. When asked where he ranked, he said, "Nowhere near those guys," although he had been the NBA scoring leader for two straight years. One day during the offseason, Durant sent out a post on Twitter that he missed playing flag football. When a fan told him where a game was going on, Durant drove there and jumped right in, with a bunch of kids in Stillwater, Oklahoma. Rather than put on a show like James, when Durant became a restricted free agent he recognized that Oklahoma City matched his laid-back style, and decided he would try to win a title there. Durant is the product of someone taking him at an early age and instilling the importance of humility. This is rare.

Few high school players come to college with humility. There are many qualities I like in young people today better than I did twenty-five years ago. But one of the big changes I don't like is the lack of humility. Much of that stems from a change within the parents. Rather than instill incredible discipline from an early age, they instead keep telling their children how great they are with what I call undeserved praise, building them up constantly. What then happens is a train wreck when they fail. Too much praise also sets up within children an unrealistic view of themselves and unrealistic expectations for their future. In the award-winning education documentary *Waiting for "Superman,"* this statistic is reported: American students ranked No. 1 in the world in confidence, but No. 45 in the world in science. When our players arrive at the University of Louisville, what I tell them is this: "High school is over. People telling you how great you are, undeserved praise, is not going to happen here. You are going to get praise for your work ethic; you're going to get praise for a job well done; but you're going to understand, you're going to deserve that praise, and you're going to have to earn it. You're going to carry yourself in such a way that when somebody gives you that praise, you'll pass it along to your teammates." We spend a lot of time on humility.

Junior Bridgeman is a former All-American at Louisville and a former star with the Milwaukee Bucks. Though he was a sixth man, he was so respected around the league that he became president of the NBA Players Association and his No. 2 was retired by the Bucks. He came in and talked to our Louisville players about his beginnings in business, and it really opened their eyes. Junior was an established NBA player with a role in union leadership, but during his time away from the court, he already was getting involved in his next business move: the restaurant industry. Junior not only bought a handful of restaurants during his playing days, but he went to work inside them. He worked at the cash register. He worked the drive-through window. He worked the grills and learned the business from the ground up, inside out. Can you imagine an NBA player today jumping into work in a fast-food restaurant, outside of a publicity stunt? But the humility that enabled him to do that has paved the way for his success since. He has become one of the most successful executives not only in the state of Kentucky, but the nation. If you look at the *Forbes* list of the nation's richest African Americans, he ranks in the top twenty, right along with Oprah Winfrey, Magic Johnson, Jay-Z, and Bill Cosby. And he is one of the humblest people I know, a prime example of someone humbly working to learn his profession and reach his potential, and you know he is going to sustain that success.

Bridgeman said he was impressed at meeting Walmart founder Sam Walton for the first time. He wasn't sure what to expect of such a successful person. He was surprised when Walton drove up in an older pickup truck and emerged wearing jeans and a flannel shirt. Bridgeman immediately liked him because of his lack of arrogance and pretense.

Bob Russell, Bridgeman's close friend and pastor at Southeast Christian Church in Louisville, one of the nation's largest congregations, calls Bridgeman one of the humblest people he knows, particularly for a person at such a high level of leadership. Russell fits the same description. He helped to build one of the nation's ten largest churches, but shies away from the limelight whenever he can. When asked to write the story of the success at Southeast, which began small and now has more than 22,000 members attending every weekend at four campuses, the title was, "When God Builds a Church." It certainly wasn't titled, "When Bob Russell Built a Church," though ministers around the world seek his counsel on leadership and ministry. Bob said one of the most impressive examples of humility he ever encountered was the popular preacher Billy Graham. During a series of sermons at Papa John's Cardinal Stadium at the University of Louisville in 2001, Russell was among a group of local ministers asked to pray with Graham before Graham would go out to speak. One night, a local seminary professor was invited in to pray with the group. Russell overheard Graham talking to the professor, and before the group left heard him say, "I wish I had more time. I'd like to ask you some more questions." Russell was amazed that the most famous evangelist in the world would humbly ask questions of a professor. "One of the marks of humility is openness to teaching," Russell told his congregation in a sermon about the subject.

Russell said he often uses the example of Jim Collins, business consultant, when talking about the importance of humility in leadership. In his best-selling book *Good to Great,* Collins distinguishes between Level 5 leaders (the highest level) with one level below, by noting that Level 5 leaders are more likely to put the interests of the company ahead of themselves and stay behind the scenes, while Level 4 leaders, who are just as gifted, have more interest in recognition. Level 4 leaders included bigger names, such as Lee Iacocca. In his Level 5 list were people you probably hadn't heard of, like Darwin Smith of Kimberly-Clark. Yet these executives, whose names were more obscure, were leading companies that outperformed others and, just as important, doing it over an extended time.

Here's what Collins writes of Level 5 leaders:

"They are somewhat self-effacing individuals who deflect adulation, yet who have an almost stoic resolve to do absolutely whatever it takes to make the company great, channeling their ego needs away from themselves and into the larger goal of building a great company. It's not that Level 5 leaders have no ego or self-interest. Indeed, they are incredibly ambitious— but their ambition is foremost for the institution and its greatness, not for themselves."

We see the same principles in sports, with players who are more humble and less concerned with celebrity becoming the ones who are able to sustain success—

true success, contentment, and happiness—over a longer time.

Contrast the stories of Terrell Owens, Mike Tyson, and others with Nazr Mohammed. Here's a young man who was very humble from the start, who knew that whatever he was going to get he was going to have to work hard to achieve. He lived very conservatively, like any union employee might live, and now for the next twenty or thirty years of his life he'll live very happily because of his playing career, despite never making a huge salary by NBA standards. Humble people understand that no matter how much success they are having, it won't last forever, and they need to plan for their future.

There are so many examples of humility being a catalyst to greater success and happiness. For some, like LeBron James, it is like breaking through a barrier. We had a cross-country All-American from the University of Louisville named Wesley Korir. Wesley grew up in very humble circumstances in Kenya. He ran five miles to school, one way, every day, and he ran home and back at lunchtime. When he showed up to run his first marathon after college, the Chicago Marathon, they asked him if he was an elite runner, and he said yes. But because he had never run a marathon before, they made him start in the back with all the recreational runners. He did as he was told, and still finished fifth. The organizers were falling all over themselves to take care of him after the race. He won the Los Angeles Marathon twice, but one day he decided he was taking too much pride in the races he'd already won. He called a local reporter to say he wanted to give away his medals because they were becoming an obstacle to him, and he felt his pride in them was somehow a danger to him. With the help of a local minister, he distributed those medals to young runners to serve as inspiration. Having made that symbolic act, Wesley returned to his roots, got back to the basics of his success, and won an even greater prize—the Boston Marathon—in 2012. His story illustrates the value of examining yourself honestly, recognizing when pride is crowding out humility, and having the discipline to remain humble amid success. We may not all give away our trophies and championship rings, but we need to mentally take them off before moving forward, and focus more on what it took to attain them.

Another Louisville athlete, Tony Stallings, was a football running back for the Cardinals who found some notoriety after his playing career by winning the *King of the Jungle* reality show on Animal Planet. But Tony could not give up his football dream, to the detriment of his family and his future. He even tells about camping out at the Cleveland Browns' training complex to try to get them a copy of his game tape when his electricity and heat were being shut off at home, leaving his wife and child stranded back in Louisville. He finally accepted an end to his football career, and came back to Louisville and began a job going door-to-door for the local cable company. It pained him every time he was recognized. One Sunday, the sermon at his church was on the subject of humility, and he realized how much his pride was hurting him. Having learned that lesson, he relaunched his acting and modeling career. He opened a gym to train others. In 2010 he landed a role in a movie titled *Courageous*, an independent church-produced film that eventually grossed $34 million and became for a time in early 2012 the nation's top-selling DVD. Tony has since moved to Los Angeles where he is a minister, acting instructor, and actor. "It wasn't until I let go of that pride that something changed for me," he said. "It wasn't just that I needed to be humbled. I needed to accept that humility."

What does true humility look like? Dakota Meyer is a Marine sergeant from Columbia, Kentucky. On September 8, 2009, in Afghanistan, he heard over the radio that some of his team was under fire. He climbed on a gun truck, got another Marine to drive, and rode in to meet about fifty Taliban fighters. During a six-hour firefight, he turned the tide of that battle by himself, according to military accounts. His citation later would read that Meyer "saved 36 Marines and soldiers and recovered the bodies of his fallen brothers. Four separate times he fought the kilometer up into the heart of a deadly U-shaped ambush. During the fight he killed at least eight Taliban, personally evacuated twelve friendly wounded, and provided cover for another twenty-four Marines and soldiers to escape likely death at the hands of a numerically superior and determined foe."

When he got the call that he had been awarded the military's highest honor, the Medal of Honor, which no living Marine then held, his immediate response was, "I don't want it," because although he had saved many Americans, he could not save members of his own team. He explained, "I thought of myself as a failure. I couldn't even get one member of my own team out alive. I lost them. They were the closest people to me in life." It took the president of the United States and some other military leaders to convince him that the award was about more than him, and that he should see the responsibility that receiving it would entail. On the day the president was scheduled to call and tell him of the award, Meyer had to work at his construction job in Kentucky. White House aides told him that he might have to wait for several hours for the call, and he told them that he had to go to work, that he was part of a construction crew that needed him. When the president finally caught up with him on the phone, Meyer was at his construction site.

The person with true humility does not see himself

as a lone fighter. People with humility see themselves as part of something bigger. At Louisville, we talk to our players a lot about "team ego." Sergeant Meyer saw himself only as part of a team. He rejected the title of hero when first offered to him, because he felt he had let down his team.

Players with humility lift up the teammates around them. Derek Fisher, talking about Kevin Durant, said, "His attitude affects everything in this organization." A star player without humility can hurt a team. I am hoping that Terrence Williams, a player who is like a son to me, will find humility in a big way. Terrence came from a difficult childhood and often likes to be the center of attention. I've always felt that when the lesson of humility kicks in for him, he will explode onto the scene. He has tremendous talent and did many great things for us, and that's my wish for him. On the other extreme, Francisco Garcia was as humble a person as you will meet, and he spent a great deal of time trying to lift up others. When we went to the Final Four in 2005 and a reporter asked Francisco what he was most proud of regarding the team, he said, "I'm proud of how humble we are." I guess that's possible! If you're going to have pride, pride in your humility is probably not a bad thing.

For me, this subject is woven through every other discussion, whether it is about success, leadership, dealing with adversity, sustaining prosperity, or happiness. Whether it comes through painful life experience or even through reading about the experiences of others, it is a lesson that is better learned sooner than later. With humility, you are better able to enjoy and understand success, and you are better able to examine and handle failure.

I couldn't enjoy the Final Four with Providence College in 1987 because of the death of my infant son and I was watching my family suffer. In 1996 at Kentucky, we were in such a cocoon that it was nearly impossible to enjoy. The one thing I wanted to make sure of when Louisville went to the Final Four in 2012 was that everybody around us would enjoy the experience. We started the whole thing in New York with the Big East Tournament, where everybody had a great time and celebrated that victory. So we went into the NCAA Tournament with the right mind-set and we were determined to keep it. In 2013, there was pressure. We were expected to win the tournament. The journey, as you'll read in these pages, was filled with obstacles. But when we won the title, and stood there with "One Shining Moment" playing, all of us were able to look around and know that the title wouldn't have happened without so many others contributing. I saw my players, and so many families, and my own family on the court with me, and it was truly a time to celebrate. This time, winning the championship was a profoundly humbling experience, thinking about what these young men had accomplished, where they had come from, and how hard they'd worked. I marveled at what they were able to do.

Humility stops you from overestimating your own significance and it enables you to accept, understand, and live with failures and learn from them constructively. Humility teaches us that our successes, like our failures, are not earthshaking, and are more to be viewed as accomplishments shared with others or shortfalls to be improved upon, nothing more, nothing less. Humble people always handle adversity so much better because they understand who they are. It's not the clothes they wear, the cars they drive, the home they live in, the jewelry they put on, or the way people recognize them. So many athletes come to disappointing ends and wonder why it happened. Most often, it was a lack of humility, leading to arrogance, leading to the mistakes they made. They think they are more significant than they are and it makes them gamble with their lives and their professions. Then, when things go wrong, they lash out and blame others. Arrogant people spread around their failure with blame. Humble people share the credit of their success, and accept their failures with courage and character.

As a young coach, I made an exhaustive study of Vince Lombardi's coaching philosophies and techniques.

When Lombardi was breaking into coaching, as an assistant to the legendary Red Blaik at Army, one of his jobs was to take the film of that week's game to General Douglas MacArthur at his home in the Waldorf Towers in New York City. Can you imagine the insight in that room? During his farewell speech, Lombardi remembered one thing that MacArthur told him about football, but I think it is true of all sports. Lombardi said MacArthur told him, "It teaches the strong to know when they are weak, and the brave to face themselves when they are afraid, to be proud, and to be unbending in defeat, yet humble and gentle in victory, and to master ourselves before we attempt to master others, to learn to laugh yet never forget how to weep, and it gives a predominance of courage over timidity."

There's one other important lesson humility teaches. It instills a sense of gratitude, even in the midst of difficult times. Gratitude is humility's shadow. It is never far from the humble person's heart. Earlier in this chapter, I told you about Wesley Korir winning the Boston Marathon. I didn't tell you what happened after he won in Boston. Though he beat several of his countrymen in that race, Wesley was not selected by his native Kenya to run in the Olympic marathon. It was a bitter disappointment to him. It would have been to anyone. As a runner, what greater honor could there be? A prideful, arrogant person would've become angry and bitter.

Wesley, however, proclaimed himself content. "I won the Boston Marathon," he said. "I told myself, Olympics or not, I would be grateful."

After being rejected for the Olympics, Wesley did what humble people do amid disappointment. He went back to work, training at home and working on projects for his Kenyan Kids Foundation, which included the completion of a hospital in his home village that he had been working to fund. At the very moment the Opening Ceremonies were taking place in London, Wesley was back in Kenya, presiding over the opening of that hospital, and watching a team of medical professionals from the University of Louisville and elsewhere treat several thousand people for various ailments. The effort even resulted in lifesaving surgeries for three children. "Seeing those children smile and knowing that their lives had been saved and they were going to live," Wesley said, "was better than any gold medal." And none of it would have happened if he had been chosen for the Olympic team, at least, not at that very important moment. Because Wesley did not react with arrogance and retreat into himself out of pride, lives were saved and changed forever. Humility and gratitude leave your heart and mind open to receive unexpected blessings, even on the heels of disappointment.

Learning the lesson of humility not only can change your life, it can change the lives of others around you. It has changed my life. As we move on in this book, I will share things I've learned and mistakes I've made. Even after learning many of these lessons, there still have been difficult times, mistakes and failures. But I have handled them better and persevered despite them because of humility. It is the most important difference between those who sustain their success, and those who falter and lose it. From looking back at thirty-five years of coaching, from observing the best and competing against the most talented, as well as experiencing the cruel turns of events that change one's life, I can tell you that not only is humility the key to finding lasting success, but it is the key to lasting happiness. You can wake up in the morning and understand what contentment is all about. Learning humility clearly is a lifelong process.

Bob Russell calls humility "the slippery virtue," because just when you feel like you have it, pride can come back and it can slip away from you. John Wooden said, "Talent is God given. Be humble. Fame is man-given. Be grateful. Conceit is self-given. Be careful."

Go back through history, literature, spiritual books, and this cycle is repeated throughout generations and cultures: arrogance, fall, acceptance, humility, healing. We're no different from people who came before us. I can't state enough how important a lesson this is to learn, and the importance of learning it before life forces you to, a truth that will continue to reveal itself in the coming pages.

By the end of the basketball season, I didn't have to keep writing "Humility" on the board, but I did. It set a tone for our players, who repeatedly exemplified being humble and hungry, in the midst of wins, losses, and, in the end, great praise and expectations. As I remember my players smiling in their championship moment, I know that if they can hold tight to the lessons of humility they learned in that championship season, for me it surely will be better than any title.

2

The Force of Focus

When our University of Louisville basketball team lost by thirty-one points at Providence in January of 2012, you'd have been surprised that we were able to fly home judging by the reaction in Louisville. Everyone in town thought the sky was falling. Fans were down on our players and on us as coaches. Everybody thought that we had lost our edge and were falling apart. Criticism came from all angles. We had suffered a wide range of injuries, but that didn't seem to matter. Two days after we came home, the *Courier-Journal* ran a story quoting my predecessor, Denny Crum, as saying, "Rick's got the reputation of overworking his kids." Overwork them? We had so many injuries we couldn't even have full practices most days. I even lost my focus, and confronted the writer of that story after a press conference. The external stimulus was all negative, and it was hard for us to ignore. We had won our first twelve games and climbed to No. 4 in the national polls. But at Providence, our guys had lost focus, and we had to get it back.

Whatever is happening in life, focus is the key to performance. Without it, you flounder. The trainer puts blinders on a thoroughbred racehorse so that it is not distracted from the race ahead. We are, in this time, a distracted people. You may not have suffered a blow-out loss on the road, but just the simple act of reading this book right now provides all the illustration you need for the challenge of focus. You have a hundred things that can derail you from reading these pages, starting with the phone in your pocket. Your mind may wander, someone may interrupt you, a dinner reservation might jump into your head, or one line may throw your mind onto a tangent.

The challenges are the same for me. As a basketball coach, every day there are so many things that not only can cause me stress, but can remove my focus from between the lines. When you are in season as a coach, you have to focus all of your energy on your players, your system, your strategy, your opponents, your family, and your health. From the moment you wake up, your focus and effort have to be on those areas. Everything else, all these other distractions and things that shake your focus, also take away from you excelling at what you do, and can, in fact, lead to negatives or aggravate crises already present in your life.

We have talked already about the things that cause stress and rob people of their focus and energy. The first step for many people is realizing that they are "in season." You know this mind-set. If you are a sports fan, you know the passion you expect of your favorite players, teams, and coaches when the season has begun. You expect full commitment and full effort. A great many people today need to realize that they are in season in their lives. They are between the lines.

If you are looking for a job, you are in season. If you are experiencing financial hardship, you are in season. If you have family problems or issues with your children, you are in season. If you are struggling to climb the ladder at work, you are in season. If you are in the midst of adversity, self-made or otherwise, you are in season. These issues and so many others require a between-the-lines mind-set. Between the lines, there is focus or there is failure. Those are the stakes. So many people are failing today because they are in season but living as if it is the offseason. They are failing because they cannot maintain focus.

That's why this discussion is so important. In thirty-five years of coaching, I've lost focus more times than you can compile on a stat sheet. I've also learned to maintain it through difficult circumstances, and to help young players maintain it.

Let's take a look at how focus works, using someone who is trying to find a job as an example. Here is how it looks between the lines. Let's say you're a young person and you studied your tail off in college, and you—like so very many today—can't get a job because of the economic climate. You are in season. You need to pursue this job that you want so badly, as we as a coaching staff would pursue a prized recruit. You will need to have focus, and you will need to be creative.

First and foremost, you must research. If we are pursuing a player, we find out who the influences are in the young man's life, and we do everything necessary to find out about what criteria will be most important in his decision. If you are going for a job, you automatically condition yourself to research who, specifically, is doing the hiring. Then you get creative. Let's say the person doing the hiring is a big football fan of a major university, for example, Alabama. You go get a football, and you do whatever you need to do to get the signature of that star running back at Alabama. You go to great pains or great lengths, no matter what you have to do, get up at five in the morning, drive several hours, whatever. But you get the football and you send it to the person doing the hiring with a note saying, "I would do anything to work for your company. Enclosed is an item signed by a great football player I hope you enjoy watching." That's going to pique the curiosity, not so much the gift, but the effort it took to get it. It may not be an autograph. It may not be a sports item. It may be some other gesture entirely. Whatever extra, even extraordinary, gesture you can muster, that's going to get your foot in the door. You must do something to separate yourself from everyone else going after that job. That type of innovation may be the difference between you and your competition.

I tell the story of a young coach who hid in the garage here at the University of Louisville. He wrote me a dozen letters saying he wanted to be a graduate assistant. I told him we had no job openings. One day I'm walking to my car and he jumps out, scares the hell out of me in the garage, and says, "Coach I didn't mean to startle you." It was too late for that. He then presented me with a basketball with his résumé written on it and said he'd do anything to become an assistant coach. That impressed me so much that I wound up interviewing him. Three weeks later I hired him as a graduate assistant, and today Gus Hauser is a full-time assistant coach at Louisiana Lafayette. I gave him a meeting just because I saw how hungry and passionate he was about the job. I gave another young man an opportunity for the same reason, an unknown player from Christian Academy High School who wrote me letter after letter asking for a chance to walk on to our basketball team until I relented and gave him a shot. Tim Henderson made two three-pointers in the Final Four against Wichita State to help us come back from twelve down to reach the national championship game. He went after his goal, and was rewarded by being the first of our players to get a shout-out from President Barack Obama during our White House visit.

So focus begins with knowledge and research. In basketball, we also call it scouting. Use that terminology if it helps you to keep the mind-set of being in season. Once you get your information, you go to work on it. Most people just send a résumé in, hoping to hear back from the employer at some point. And there are thousands of résumés out there. Someone wants to get into broadcasting and what do they do? They send a résumé to ESPN. But you don't send résumés to ESPN. That's the first thing anybody interested in sports broadcasting will do. You pick a different market, you research it, you work that market and then maybe you move forward.

The focused person is not content to fire off a résumé and wait. The focused person is living between the lines. As a focused person, do your research, get your foot in the door, and then plan the attack or game plan. You may have to go through the process with seven different people. But if you can go through the process five to seven times, you have a great chance of being hired, or being called in for interviews. Once your foot is in the door, that is your opportunity to showcase your passion and hunger to work for that company. Then, once you're in, you have to show how you're a team player. It can't be about "I." It can't be about the person in the mirror at all. It has to be about how you in some small way can use your passion and hunger to help the team prosper. It's all about the team. It's all about the company. Not only must you have focus, but it must be in the right place—on how you can lend yourself to help that business and team win. Recently it was reported that Harvard Business School has declined in popularity among companies hiring, because of what is being called "the Harvard arrogance." Employers related that its business school graduates were more concerned with where they were starting out than they were about helping the business they joined.

It's easy to focus on self. That is the natural inclination of people. But it is more productive to focus on the team. And it is even more important to focus on the work you must do to help the team. "There is nothing wrong with dedication and goals," the great Pete Maravich once said. "If you focus on yourself, all the lights fade away and you become a fleeting moment in life."

You will find, as you study the subject, that in some cases it is not an inability to focus that runs people off the tracks, but focusing on the wrong things.

Few athletes had greater powers of concentration than Michael Jordan. But Jordan also knew where to keep his focus. He said, "I would tell players to relax and never think about what's at stake. Just think about the basketball game. If you start to think about who is going to win the championship, you've lost your focus."

Now, we've been talking about a person who needs a job, but this is the process for anyone with any goal. This is the focused approach: research, putting forth great effort to get a foot in the door, then being the consummate team player. So many times, people lose focus and get discouraged and depressed because they allow disappointment to detract from their focus.

That was the danger for my team after our thirty-one-point loss at Providence. I had made it worse because I was upset. I sat down our starters in the second half. I wanted it to hurt. I let it hurt for a few days. I didn't pick our guys up immediately. I wanted to teach them a lesson, to restore their humility. I wanted them hungry again. They took Providence lightly. They'd lost their mental focus. The public didn't understand that I wanted them to really feel that loss. And they felt it. We all did. Even though we were amid a rash of injuries like I'd never experienced in all my years of coaching, when we started losing everything began to be criticized. People started to say I was too old. As I've mentioned, I was accused of working the players too hard. All the negative things began to pour in around us. It's hard to avoid, particularly in this age of social media. Bad news always spreads fast, and technology spreads it faster than anything. When this happens, you cannot let the negativity and disappointment infiltrate all you're trying to accomplish. That does not mean you can't alter your system or make necessary adjustments, but you cannot deviate from your main goal. Everybody loses focus when bad things happen. We all do. Some go to alcohol, others to drugs or depression. But when things are difficult, that is the time to become more focused, to dig in deeper. If you've done your research and the job offers aren't coming, you need to research it even more.

I told our team, when we were hurt and struggling and under a lot of criticism from the outside, "Look, we're going through a tough stretch. Our trainer can't wave a magic wand and make you better. But we are going to get healthier. In the meantime, we've got to hold tight, hold steady." I said in a meeting to our point guard Peyton Siva, "Everybody's second-guessing you. No different from the way they're second-guessing me as a coach. Everybody is second-guessing our recruiting. Everybody is second-guessing everything that is going on because we're losing. That's the way life is today. It is a microwave society. You can't focus on it. You have to keep your mind on what you're doing, not on what people want or what anyone is saying."

For Peyton Siva, this was a very important lesson. All his life, Peyton has been looking out for other people. He came from a rough background in Seattle. From national media accounts, the story of the thirteen-year-old Siva climbing into the family car to fish his alcoholic and suicidal father off the streets of Seattle is known chapter and verse, right down to his father throwing away the handgun he intended to use on himself with a vow to change his life. But there were other challenges.

Peyton grew up facing full-court pressure—a brother who dealt drugs, a half-sister who stole. Friends who fell by the wayside, some despite his efforts, and the story of his efforts to save his father from alcoholism, and even possible suicide, has been chronicled in national publications. Peyton tries to take care of his teammates, family, everybody—and in the case of his family has succeeded in helping them overcome these various issues. By the time Siva graduated high school, his father was coaching youth sports and using his prior transgressions as cautionary tales. His brother was working as a carpenter and his half-sister was in a trade school. I sat down with him, though, when we were in a difficult stretch of the season and reminded him that he was in season. While it is a great and even noble thing to focus on everyone else, there also comes a time to focus on the task at hand. Once he rededicated himself to school and to basketball, the season turned around for him, and he became the point guard who led us to back-to-back Final Fours and the national title.

All that seemed a distant dream in 2012 when we had lost five out of seven games in conference. Then I told our players something else, a lesson for us all. You have to remember how you will be judged. Fair or unfair, you have to understand it. At that moment, everybody believed we were mediocre. I told them you can't let outside people judge your performance. It has to be the people in our locker room, and within our coaching staff. I told them that nobody would remember the fact that we went through these tough times. I told them they would solely be judged on the final exam.

Over and over, we talked about the final exam, which for us was the NCAA Tournament. We had a dress rehearsal with the Big East Tournament. But when it came to judging us, all of that difficulty right then would be irrelevant, unless we gave in to it. This is something worth thinking about for everyone struggling to regain focus. On what will you be judged, the current difficulty, or the final result? We talked about the final exam a lot. We maintained our focus by paying attention to what we wanted to achieve at the end of the year, not by looking at our difficult circumstances, or what outsiders were saying. We gave our guys many examples of comebacks through injuries and woeful shooting.

All during that rough stretch, we used the New York Giants in the 2012 Super Bowl as an illustration. They were written off for dead when they lost four straight games in November and early December. They went almost an entire calendar month without a win. By that point, the *New York Post* and *Daily News* had both called for their coach, Tom Coughlin, to be fired. Of course, our guys knew how it ended.

The Giants had to go on the road and get through the playoffs the hard way. We told our players, "We're not going to have a highest seed. We probably will have to travel. Our fans will not be able to follow us. But look at what the Giants accomplished because they stayed focused." That season, injury-filled and frustrating as it was, turned out to be one of the greatest seasons I've had as a basketball coach. And that's because, except for one incident involving me, we never lost focus on what we had to do. That team wound up in the Final Four for one main reason—it did not lose focus down the stretch, no matter what was said or what adversity it faced.

As I have often mentioned, my philosophy is not to read local newspapers or watch evening news telecasts.

As a matter of fact, in my twelve years as coach of the University of Louisville, I have never watched an evening newscast sports report or read our hometown newspaper. But even with that type of focus and shelter of my mind, other people will come up to me, as was the case with *Courier-Journal* reporter C. L. Brown. He wrote a story addressing the accusation that I overworked my players. Well, that was ridiculous. Half the team was injured. We probably had done less hard practicing that season than any team I ever had coached, and C.L. knew that. In the first press conference after he wrote that story, I confronted him privately in the hallway, and I should not have done that. I called him later and apologized, and I said, "C.L. you're doing your job. I shouldn't have lost focus on mine." My job is not to answer my critics, and that's something I pride myself on, not answering the Internet or newspaper articles or TV things, because that's when you lose focus. When you get caught up in what people are saying about you, true or untrue, you lose focus on what is going on between the lines. No amount of answering my critics was going to get my injured players healthy or make my team execute better. Plain and simple, you cannot get distracted. Criticism, or any form of negative behavior, will make you lose focus and you must avoid paying too much attention to it. Allowing your focus to drift to negativity or criticism will put you on the defensive. It will get you pointing fingers and take away from the job you are doing.

The most famous time I lost focus in season was when I made a statement I consider humorous today. When I was coaching the Celtics, I told Boston fans that Larry Bird, Kevin McHale, and Robert Parrish "are not walking through that door." That has been repeated and referenced so many times with so many commentators that it is absolutely hysterical. Even though I laugh at it today, it wasn't funny at the time. It was a sign that I certainly had lost focus. When you change everything because of your critics, you are losing focus, and when you answer them you are losing focus. Leave your critics isolated. Stay focused on your journey only.

Sometimes we not only need to escape from disappointment, but from the big successes. In coaching, so many times great things happen and then suddenly you delegate more, or take more time off, or get away from the things that have brought success and soon you find you have lost your way. You cannot become distracted by success, and losing focus happens just as much through prosperity as it does adversity.

No modern athlete is better known for his powers of focus and concentration than Tiger Woods. His ability to block everything else out on the course, including his playing partners, became the stuff of legend. He credited his ability to focus for his powers of handling stress, and for his ability to perfect his swings through practice, then repetition. But Woods also serves as the ultimate lesson in not handling success. His life ran badly off course as his fame and fortune rose beyond that of any athlete in the world. Today, he is rebuilding the focus of his prior greatness, but he still is paying the price for his inability to handle success. Watching him, even after all of his troubles, practicing under the lights at 5:30 A.M., shows you that he is intent on getting back to top form. It signals to me an athlete who is serious about returning to the top of his game, and I expect him to do it in time.

There's another way that success can steal your focus. Many people have success in one area and then begin to reach out into endeavors in other areas and shift their focus from those things that brought them great success. Some people can do this successfully. The Frank Sinatras of the world can be award-winning singers and actors. Will Smith is another one, or Bette Midler, Cher, or Justin Timberlake. But for every person who can manage success over a variety of endeavors, there are dozens who can't, and who wind up drawing their focus from where it should be. Shaquille O'Neal was a great basketball player and had some success as an actor, but wanted to try rapping and spread himself thin on all fronts. So many people try to leave their skill sets and walk away from what they do well. There's nothing wrong with learning another area, but sometimes the price is losing focus on what you do best.

Several years back, leaders at Google were looking to broaden their horizons. They had the most dominant Internet search engine in the world, but they wanted to take that success to other areas. One of the people they asked for advice was Apple founder Steve Jobs. In his biography of Jobs, Walter Isaacson says Jobs went in and told the leaders at Google, "What are the five products you want to focus on? Get rid of the rest because they are dragging you down. They're turning you into Microsoft. They're causing you to turn out products that are adequate but not great." Jobs was well known for his ability to focus and, according to one colleague, "turn off the noise around him." Jobs also said this: "Focus is about saying no." He had many opportunities to create new products come his way every day. He spent his time and energy only on those very best ideas, the ones about which he was most passionate.

That's a frequent mistake people make in business. The successful pizza chain wants to go into sandwiches. The successful soft drink company wants to tinker with formulas.

It's not just a mistake made on grand scales. We can make it every day in our own work. One mistake I've made as a coach is putting in our entire system at the beginning of the season. We'd install it all—our press, zone, man defense, run, and jumps, put in everything at the beginning—then I'd start working on the parts. But the parts weren't really good. They'd grade out at a C or a B, and they'd start to become an A sometime in January or early February. Well, that was all right because my whole goal was to get ready for March. But increasingly in life, and at work, the problem is that you've got to have some parts operating at Bs and As immediately. Today, you may not be able to get where you want to go, because of the way you're judged, if you don't get there quicker. To do that, we need to spend time working on our strengths to make them as good as they can be.

A *Harvard Business Review* study by Tony Schwartz and Catherine McCarthy confirmed the value of honing your strengths. They reported: "People tap into the energy of the human spirit when their everyday work and activities are consistent with what they value most and with what gives them a sense of meaning and purpose. If the work they're doing really matters to them, they typically feel more positive energy, focus better, and demonstrate greater perseverance."

On a smaller level, this means making sure that you give as much time to the facets of your work that you are good at, or leave you fulfilled, as those parts that leave you drained. It doesn't mean you shouldn't work on your weaknesses, or ignore them. But the study found that those workers who spent more time in their "sweet spot" actually became more productive in their time working in other areas, as well.

None of that, of course, can happen without a plan. Nearly all the literature on the subject says the same thing—focus is intentional. It does not just happen, you have to consciously plan for it and learn to achieve it. It always involves prioritizing the things that are important to you. It has to be a deliberate effort. Human nature is to follow distraction. Every day as coaches, we make choices, we have a plan for the day, and within those plans are more detailed plans. Every practice, we know how many minutes we are going to spend on each drill, on each session, based on what we have determined is most important for the team. Knowing what you should be focused on, and when, is an important part of recognizing when your focus is slipping. Part of prioritizing, planning, and scheduling is being on time. If you can't be punctual, it's likely you have too much going on, and that robs you of the ability to focus.

Another part of focus is being healthy. Since I have been a coach, our strategy has always been to fatigue our opponents at some point in the second half of games, so that they will just give in physically and mentally to the pressure we apply. Sometimes great teams don't give in and you just have to out-execute them, but the effects of fatigue and pressure are documented, and those are the reasons we try to do what we do offensively and defensively. The team that goes down and throws up a quick shot is not going to fatigue its opponent. The team that takes a good shot, forcing the other team to play defense, is going to fatigue the opponent.

The same principle applies with focus. If you become fatigued, you lose it. It's well known that I always have made our coaches stay in great shape. Take a look at the tale of the tape. Marvin Menzies lost forty pounds working for us at Louisville. Chris Wallace lost a hundred pounds in Boston. Tim Fuller lost forty pounds, Kevin Keatts twenty-five pounds, Scotty Davenport sixty pounds. With all of these men, you could see their self-esteem rise because their physical condition was improving. One reason I had them do that is to set an example. If we are out of shape as a coaching staff, how can we demand it of our players? But another reason is that being in great shape lends to better focus.

Getting enough rest, proper nutrition, exercise, all of these bring out your best and are proven to promote better concentration. Remember, one major cause of stress among Americans is concern about health. Physical conditioning is a major factor in that. Chris Christie, governor of New Jersey, is widely recognized as one of the more gifted politicians on either side of the aisle. Yet one of the reasons I believe he did not make a presidential run in 2012 was that he felt his weight was a major issue. How could you do the type of campaigning necessary if you're not in the right condition? It's not possible, you'll become fatigued, say the wrong thing. Your behavior under the influence of stress will be negative. If you are not in good physical condition, your ability to focus is compromised and your breaking point is going to be much quicker than others. It will be fascinating to see, in the wake of his gastric band weight loss surgery, what changes Christie will experience in his life. He told NBC's Brian Williams after the surgery, "I needed to take a more significant step to try to get my weight under control so that I could have a really active next half of my life."

Weight is an issue that receives a great deal of attention in American life. Walk into any bookstore and you'll find an entire section on diet and weight loss strategies. Less prominent but no less important is the role of sleep in good health, and focus. In their piece for the *Harvard Business Review*, Schwartz and McCarthy profiled a thirty-seven-year-old executive from Ernst & Young. He was working twelve- to fourteen-hour days, felt exhausted all the time, struggled to engage with his family, and found that he was eating and sleeping poorly. He did a handful of things that changed his life and led to more focus. He set an earlier bedtime and stopped drinking alcohol. Both of those increased his level of rest, and as a result he felt more motivated to exercise, which he began to do every morning. In two months, he lost fifteen pounds. He began to make time to sit down with his family for breakfast, and even though he continued to work long hours, he found ways to renew himself along the way, including getting away from his desk for lunch and a short walk each morning and afternoon.

These simple things, rest, exercise, diet, automatically led him to take other actions that improved his focus. Schwartz and McCarthy studied the habits of workers at Wachovia Bank, and found that those who set a designated bedtime and stuck to it, who ate smaller meals and took part in some exercise, and who took brief but regular breaks throughout the day were more productive and focused than their counterparts who did not. I'm at my worst as a basketball coach when I don't get the correct sleep. It's extremely important. For me, what I have found helps at night is not turning on the television but reading. If I read a chapter before I go to bed, I sleep much better.

Another important part of maintaining focus is taking time away, whether in short segments during the day or in taking away extended times when you are not in season. Studies show that most people's best work comes in ninety-minute to two-hour segments, broken up by brief breaks. Longer breaks are important, too. It is very important that you get away from your everyday stress. I take two weeks a year, go to Saratoga and Del Mar, and get completely away from basketball. You need time to unwind, relax, and truly stay away from your work. When the season ended this past year, my goal was to take each of my children on a mini-vacation. The idea was to be with them, to give them undivided attention, and to say thank you for sacrificing. It's important that, in the process of focus and work, you don't deprive your family of time with you, or yourself of time with them. Spending that time with your family when you are out of season also allows you to avoid any feeling of guilt that you're taking away from them when you have to focus so much on work. It helps you stay focused when it is time to stay focused.

It's important here to draw a distinction between focus and obsession. That's not what we're talking about when we discuss focus. People who are obsessed burn out more easily. People who are focused rejuvenate themselves and move forward. People who are obsessed will eventually become fatigued and falter. An unhealthy focus on work to the exclusion of all else is not the answer.

Focus, then, is a discipline. From the time you wake up, it must be a conscious effort. Like the bank executive or the ballplayer, you must develop a routine that fosters focus. As coaches, we spend years developing and refining these routines. These are the things you turn to when you find that you are distracted or that your focus is slipping away. They help you realize when you have gotten into habits that rob you of focus. One of the biggest mistakes I've made is that I've allowed our players to play pickup basketball. It's undisciplined. Defense is not played. Passing is not at a premium. Team basketball is not at a premium. Winning is not at a premium. It takes away from all the things we try to teach all year in practice. Why would I allow that to happen? So I've totally taken pickup basketball out of the spring and summer and early fall. I let them play one-on-one because they've been through the drills. But you cannot keep creating bad habits on top of each other. So you have to have a positive routine every day. I call it your discipline, and people lose that from time to time. We know our routines, and how to create routines for successful basketball players and teams. I tell our players, "There's Friday and Saturday, and then there's the other days of the week. You have to understand the difference between those."

After our humbling loss at Providence, our team went to Pittsburgh and won a game between two teams in must-win situations on an ESPN College GameDay stage. Even had the stakes not been so high, winning those games where opposing fans spend the whole day in the arena getting fired up for the ESPN cameras is extremely difficult. But our guys had refocused, and we would not lose that focus for the rest of the season.

That team, of course, went to a Final Four, whereas I had a team several years back with two NBA Draft Lottery picks that did not advance past the Elite Eight. But there were different mind-sets within the team. For those guys back then, if you had a morning practice, it was totally different from an afternoon practice. But the makeup of the individuals on the Final Four team was such that they knew the difference between when to focus and when to back off. It's your routine. You have to understand how to establish your routine the right way. So many of us establish bad routines—staying up too late, not getting up early, and eating the wrong food. We are busy, but we are busy at the wrong things. We create poor habits. "Don't mistake activity for achievement," John Wooden said. Being focused is about creating positive habits.

Ted Williams was one of the greatest hitters who ever lived. He spoke of seeing a baseball right down to the individual stitches as it was approaching home plate. What you did not see when you watched Williams at the plate were the countless hours he spent not only practicing hitting, but studying the craft and science of hitting. After his playing days, he wrote a book about hitting that still is used extensively today. Williams said that an average hitter swinging at a good pitch to hit is better than a great hitter swinging at a bad pitch. Basketball is no different. A good shooter taking a great shot is better than a great shooter taking a bad one. Using the principles of focus, you can determine for yourself the best pitches to hit, the job to pursue, the project to devote the bulk of your time to, the approach to take for success in life and in work.

The story of Russ Smith's emergence as one of the nation's best players is one that is well known from our 2013 championship run. Russ's rise is solely attributable to developing his ability to focus. Russ's attention span was maybe the shortest on our team when he arrived. I famously gave him the nickname "Russdiculous," and he earned it. He was a nervous breakdown waiting to happen. As a coach, watching him on the court was a harrowing experience. The fans loved it, because Russ is full-speed, all the time. He thought about three things on the court: scoring, scoring, and scoring. It was fun to watch, not so fun to coach. In some ways, Russ's game was misunderstood by scouts and commentators. Though he put up a lot of shots, Russ was not being a selfish player. He honestly thought he was doing the best thing for the team, and in many cases, he was. I needed him to be an offensive catalyst during times when we were having trouble scoring, and his ability to drive and get to the free throw line saved us many times. But after our five-overtime loss at Notre

Dame, it was crucial that Russ Smith change his mindset. After mismanaging three straight timeouts offensively and defensively, I finally called timeout and said Russ, I'm going to make this easy for you. You've screwed up the last three timeouts. Peyton Siva is out of the game. I'm going to put four guys on the baseline, and there are fifteen seconds left. You are not to start your drive until there are six seconds left. I made him repeat it back to me to make sure he got it. So we get in the game and I'm calling out every second.

"Fifteen, fourteen, thirteen. Remember Russ, don't go until six!" I screamed.

He's weaving back and forth. Ten, nine, then all of a sudden—he's ten feet behind the college three-point line—at nine seconds he heaves up an impossible jump shot, and I go ballistic. The guys on the team can't fathom why he would do that. I go berserk. I don't know why he did it. He comes to the sideline and I ask if there is something wrong with him. I yell to our team doctor to get out there and give him medication. I say what do you have to say for yourself, Russ?

He looks at me and says, "You're having a bad day, Coach, give me a hug."

But from that point on, he really started to lock in and pay attention. He buried himself in scouting reports. I explained to him that now that he was scoring at such a high rate and had become such a weapon, teams were going to key on him to try to take him away, and he needed to realize when that was happening and in those times become a facilitator on offense rather than a scorer.

Russ is a textbook example of what happens when someone has great desire and acquires great focus. He went from an unheralded high school player to a third-team college All-American, and after deciding to return to school for his senior year, has a chance to be one of the nation's top college basketball players in 2014. But it wasn't until he harnessed the force of focus that his game went from sideshow to serious. During our championship run, Russ devoured scouting reports, not only offensively but on defense. He picked his spots. His shooting percentage increased. He opened NCAA Tournament play by setting a single-game tournament record with eight steals. Heading into our game against Duke in the Midwest Regional Final, I reminded him that Duke probably was going to try to take him out of the game offensively and that he needed to look to pass the ball. Russ answered me, "I've got it, Coach. I know how to play this game now." And he does.

He went from a player who sent me to my knees in prayer every time he touched the ball to a player you can trust with any situation. He didn't have his best shooting or scoring games in the Final Four in Atlanta, but in the championship game against Michigan he made one of the biggest passes of the game, driving into the lane to dish to Luke Hancock for a three that put us up by ten points late. The lesson of Russ Smith is that you may have a lot of tools and even talent, and you might even be using them to gain a certain level of success. But if you're looking for serious success, you've got to harness the force of focus.

Like Russ with the scouting report, and like the executive from Ernst & Young who changed his sleep and work schedules, we must go about creating the small habits that form a routine that allows us to focus. Some have begun the habit of making themselves go thirty minutes between checking e-mail or messages. Set a block of ninety minutes and determine to work solidly through it. For others, it may be identifying the areas that cause distraction throughout the day, or, as Russ did, simply turning your focus in a different and more beneficial direction. Whatever the case, focus will not happen on its own. It must be deliberately created.

There are going to be personal crises. There are going to be health issues. There are going to be distractions. But once you go between the lines, while those issues won't go away, you have to leave them behind. Even in my personal crisis at the University of Louisville—when I faced an attempt to extort money from me—between the lines I had to stay totally into what I had to do, because that was my job. Here was a case of someone seeking to apply high pressure and deliberate distraction at moments that person determined would be the most important of the season. They calculated extortion attempts to times when they thought they could do the most damage—when the most was at stake. Here also lies a lesson. When the stakes are the biggest is when the challenges to focus can be the most difficult and the most costly. Always during those times, I tried to realize that the important thing remained my responsibility to my players and the University of Louisville. I would save my problems for my own time. But nothing good would come of helping me solve those problems if I wavered in my performance and we lost games. Quite simply, if you get distracted from doing your job, you can't perform. And remember this— there is very little sympathy out there for people who cannot perform. And I do mean very little. I've seen baseball players go into slumps and despite being the most popular players on their teams, some of them even the most popular in the history of the game, they will get booed if they don't perform. Slumps are not tolerated. They just are not.

Focus is more than just a sports cliché. Focus is a powerful force in overcoming adversity and reaching goals. As we move forward in the coming chapters, we will deal in detail with areas that can rob people of focus, and with how to perform in the midst of them.

Muhammad Ali said, "Often it isn't the mountains ahead that wear you out, it's the little pebble in your shoe." We'll take a look at some of the pebbles, and talk about handling the mountains. In the end, performance is your greatest ally in dealing with adversity, and focus is your greatest weapon in achieving that performance.

3

The Trap of Technology

Here's the scene: I'm with a recruit and we're speaking, and his phone is constantly going off. Maybe he glances down, or I can sense by his demeanor that he wants to glance down at the texts or e-mails coming in. And it doesn't stop. Already, I don't want to coach this guy—no matter how good he is—because I know that he's going to be constantly distracted.

Technology is a valuable tool for us all, but we cannot allow it to creep between the lines. And it has. It has taken the front of distracting influences in all walks of life. Many people are slaves to technology. If you can read four or five pages in this book without looking at your phone, stopping to read an e-mail, or checking for a text message, I believe you are in a small minority of people today. Certainly, most young people I deal with cannot sit long enough to read a single chapter. Many adults cannot. One of the greatest obstacles to your focus and ability to concentrate and succeed is the phone in your pocket, or the computer, laptop, or tablet on your desk. Technology can derail entire days—and for many people, it does.

Diagnoses of Attention Deficit Hyperactivity Disorder have skyrocketed in recent years, as has the prescribing of various drugs to treat it. *Psychology Today* published a story reporting that a new fad among Ivy League college–bound students is to snort Adderall, an amphetamine prescribed for ADHD. The *New York Times* reported that kids snort the drug in powder form to give them a "tunnel focus." That enhanced ability to focus enables them to do well on tests like the SAT. The fact that students are willing to abuse Adderall shows the performance value of laser focus, which was discussed in the previous chapter. But this is a dangerous trend. At least one study, at the University of California-Berkeley, links the use of stimulants for ADHD to serious drug abuse later in life.

All of this is evidence that the ability to concentrate is slipping away, and the phone in your hand—the technology of our society—is one of the biggest reasons. Test yourself right now. For the next fifteen minutes, challenge yourself to read the following pages with no technological interruption. If you can't, or if you find yourself with a stronger than natural urge to grab your phone or look at your e-mail, recognize that compulsion for what it is: your brain having been trained not to focus. Do you recognize the danger in that? If your favorite basketball player were texting from the bench during a big game, you'd be furious. Yet millions of Americans are doing that very thing every day. As we established in the last chapter, the ability to focus, and to focus on the right things, is an essential building block of success. If you find yourself unable to concentrate on the most important things in your life for longer stretches, examine the effect that technology has had on you. I firmly believe that people who recognize this and develop a strategy for dealing with it will immediately give themselves an edge over most people in professional life in this country. It's that important.

The average American worker wastes just over two hours of an eight-hour workday on nonwork activity, according to a survey by Salary.com and AmericaOnline, and nearly 45 percent of that is time spent surfing the Internet—almost an hour per day, per person.

Think about that. The state of Vermont did think about it. In 2010, Vermont government officials decided to look into how much productivity was being lost by state employees surfing the Web during work hours. They installed a new Web-monitoring program on state computers, and the results were breathtaking, but not surprising. The state human resources office reported that its employees were squandering the equivalent of fifty-seven full-time positions every week, or almost 120,000 employee work hours over the course of the year.

The most infamous example came in the Securities and Exchange Commission of the federal government. As the financial crisis in this country was raging at its worst, high-level SEC officials were found to be accessing pornography and other nonwork items on their government computers. One senior attorney was found to have been accessing pornographic sites for eight hours per day. Another official tried to access porn sites 1,600 times in a two-week period and had hours of images saved on her hard drive. "Ironically," ABC News reported, "the [government] report says most of these cases began in 2008, just as the financial system began to collapse. The same SEC officers who should have been safeguarding the economy were instead spending their working hours surfing the Internet for pornography, and the problem hasn't stopped."

Frankly, some of the statistics on time Americans spend on social networks are so large that they're hard to grasp. Here's one that isn't. According to a Mashable/ *USA Today* report, Americans spend twice as much time on Facebook as they do exercising. And the younger the age, the worse the effects. The average college student spends three hours a day checking social sites. According to the same *USA Today* report, the grade point average of college students who regularly use Facebook is a full point lower than their peers who do not. That alone, without any other evidence, should be enough to make a student take a hard look at how online time is spent. It certainly illustrates the negative effect of social media.

The *USA Today* report found that American workers are interrupted once every 10.5 minutes by things like e-mails, instant messages, text messages, or Tweets. Once interrupted, it takes an average of 23 minutes for them to get back on task. It estimates that social media usage is costing the American economy $650 billion per year—more than the value of Google, Chevron, and Chase Manhattan combined.

Now here's the sobering question. If that level of online time wasting is costing businesses that much money, how much is it costing you? The subject of technology— how we use it, how it is changing us, and how it is changing the way we think, interact, and learn—is one of the least discussed and most important topics of our time.

Don't misunderstand me; I am not against technology. I was recognized for being one of the first to really push the boundaries of the use of video in coaching. Everyone uses it now, but in its infancy, we used it more than anyone, and derived a great advantage. I should stop here and talk about the wonderful outpouring of support from social media that Kevin Ware received after his broken leg on national television against Duke. Kevin returned to Twitter after his surgery mainly to put a stop to fake accounts claiming to be him asking for money and other support. What happened next, though, was amazing. Pro athletes and celebrities and fans from all over the nation reached out to Kevin with kind words of support and encouragement, and it was a great thing for Kevin. Technology in itself isn't bad, nor is social media use. But it is dangerous, and so easy to let slide out of control. Manti Te'o, the outstanding Notre Dame linebacker who was duped into an online relationship by a person pretending to be a woman who did not exist, is an extreme example of how social media can cost a person far more than it benefits him. The MTV program *Catfish* chronicles the phenomenon of people who fall into online relationships, then learn later that the person they were corresponding with turns out to be much different from his or her online persona. It's a metaphor for the danger of the Web today. It looks great and stimulates our minds, but spend too much time with it, and you wind up with something that is not at all what you were setting out to find.

Technology as a tool is powerful and positive, but technology as a distraction, particularly when it comes to the Internet, is perhaps the single greatest obstacle to focus in modern life. Many people today need to put their lives into airplane mode—this very minute. In airplane mode phones are on but cannot receive calls and text messages. If your phone is on, take it out, switch it to airplane mode, and take a few minutes to see if you can focus on the words in this single chapter until the end. Many people cannot. Most of my players cannot. We are losing that ability. *Psychology Today* reports that at least 9 percent of school-age kids in this country have been diagnosed with attention deficit disorders of some kind and are being medicated for it. Other countries are reporting similar increases, though there's an interesting exception. In France, the rate of these diagnoses is far lower than it is in this country, and there's a reason. Psychologists there are treating attention deficit disorders largely as social problems, while also paying close attention to nutritional causes, rather than assuming they are primarily medical issues. And the role of technology in all of it cannot be ignored. A 2010 study published by the journal *Pediatrics* linked television and video games with subsequent attention problems, and the Internet is like television on steroids, with all of the interactive lure of video games.

On a recent recruiting trip in Washington, D.C., I was watching an AAU game in the front row with some of the most highly recognized coaches in America. One of the coaches called a thirty-second timeout and I looked around and everyone was immediately texting, looking at Twitter, or otherwise checking their phones. I stood up and said, "Will you guys look at yourselves? You can't even get through a thirty-second timeout without looking at your phone." Villanova coach Jay Wright laughed and said, "You're right. It's unbelievable."

I get it. I've fallen for the trap, too. But during a time in which evaluating players is the most crucial part of our jobs and missing a play or two could make a major difference, coaches still can't keep their phones in their pockets. It's addictive.

Nicholas Carr's book *The Shallows: What the Internet Is Doing to Our Brains* was a finalist for the Pulitzer Prize. In it, he writes, "The natural state of the human brain . . . is one of distractedness." Of technology, he goes on to say, "Dozens of studies by psychologists, neurobiologists, educators, and Web designers point to the same conclusion: when we go online, we enter an environment that promotes cursory reading, hurried and distracted thinking, and superficial learning." He characterizes the online life as "a permanent state of distractedness."

As you'll be able to tell from this chapter, this has become a fascinating and troubling subject for me. Athletes who Tweet from the locker room are fined in the NBA. Yet every day, millions of American workers do essentially the same thing from their office desks. It is time for many to reevaluate their online activity and what benefit it truly brings to them, and to hold themselves to the same high standards to which they hold their sports heroes.

ALL THAT TWITTERS IS NOT GOLD

Social media can be a wonderful thing. It helps you catch up with old friends, stay in touch with distant friends and family, and keep up with the lives of loved ones. It also can be a terrible hindrance, and for many it is. One danger of the overuse of social media is that it leads to self-promotion, which hinders humility, which erodes focus. I am anti-Twitter for coaches. I know many others in my profession are not. My son Richard, coach at Minnesota, uses it because he feels he needs to promote the program and get people talking about it. I see his point, but I'm not sure I agree with him. I do not Tweet. Our players do not Tweet.

I tend to look at the great coaches and take cues from them. Would John Wooden have been on Twitter? I don't think so. Vince Lombardi? No way. The greatest modern-day basketball coach is Mike Krzyzewski. He does not do Twitter. Neither does Bill Belichick, nor Nick Saban. Why is that? These are guys who look at it as a distraction, as a self-promotion, as taking away from the job they're doing between the lines or with recruiting. For people who every day have to deliver their motivational key as a Tweet, that kind of self-promotion can take away from the focus on the job at hand, because then you're always trying to better the Tweet, or answer the response to the Tweet, or defend your Tweet. And if someone is hired to do the Tweeting for you, then it's not genuine, so why go to the trouble? The bottom line for me is what does it accomplish? Outside of self-promotion, do you feel it enhances your program and moves you closer to your goals? That's my question.

While he was in Indianapolis for the Midwest Regional preparing his Duke basketball team to face Michigan State, Mike Krzyzewski told reporters that he didn't ban his players from social media, but that he had nothing to do with it, and his worry was its negative impact on the ability to focus.

"Through the years I'd tell our players it's like you have your own bus," he said. "You drive your bus, and you have friends and family on it. And during this time of the year, tournament time, more people want to get on the bus—in fact, sometimes they want a series of buses—and I tell our guys to try not to let other people on your bus during this time, but to try to do things like what you normally do and remember the responsibilities you have with those cell phones, Twitter, with Facebook and all the things that you can have, the Instagram, all that stuff. See, I don't have to worry about that. I don't do any of that."

I understand why media people Tweet. For them, it is essential, being in the field of distributing information. It's the same for people in marketing or public relations. But for the rest of us, very little good can come of it. A couple of years ago, we came from behind to beat Pittsburgh in a very dramatic finish, and one of their players Tweeted something derogatory about our team after the game. When he did that, he just ignited the fire for us to beat Pitt the next time we played them. Our players were burned up. Nothing good comes of it.

At the 2012 Olympics in London, a young woman from Greece, triple jumper Voula Papachristou, was sent home before the Games even began for a politically inflammatory post she put on Twitter. Think about this woman, who had worked and trained for so long to get this dream opportunity of a lifetime, and how quickly it all disappeared. Her dream was gone in 140 characters. It was absolutely needless. Nothing she could have posted would have been worth that price.

In January of 2012, high school football star Yuri Wright posted some Tweets with sexually graphic language and not only was suspended from his Don Bosco Prep football team in New Jersey, but lost a number of big-time scholarship offers. Chad Ochocinco, Mark Cuban, and Ozzie Guillen all have contributed generously to their leagues' Twitter fine funds because of posts that ran afoul of league rules. Every NBA scout tries to infiltrate the pages of prospects they're looking to draft. Players, and all of us, need to understand that everything we post can and will be used against us.

You know something is dangerous when even media professionals get into trouble using it. A Penn State media outlet Tweeted Joe Paterno's death before it happened. *USA Today* Tweeted that Diana Ross died. It meant to say that Donna Summer had passed away. NBC News, when astronaut Neil Armstrong died, Tweeted the name of singer Neil Young instead. I'm always wary of there being an instrument of communication bearing my name that I don't always control. Security is an issue on Twitter, or people impersonating you. In April of 2013, someone hacked the Associated Press's Twitter account and posted that the White House was under attack. That wasn't negligence by the AP, but it did undermine that organization's credibility.

You don't hear many stories about people doing positive things via Twitter, though I know it happens. You don't hear many stories like Kevin Ware's, about athletes benefiting from it, but you hear plenty where Twitter and the things athletes post there get them into hot water.

SOCIAL MEDIA, ANTISOCIAL BEHAVIOR

Another aspect of all this is the erosion of personal communication skills. Young people today are very expressive when it comes to written communication. They are far more emotional and willing to communicate those emotions through text or instant messages. A player will think nothing of texting "Luv u coach" to me nowadays, when we would never have said that kind of thing when I was young. But put the same player in a one-on-one setting with me, and he's awkward, uncomfortable, not sure how to look at the person across the desk or how to address him. Young people today have a very difficult time sitting in front of a human resources person and communicating their passion, because they are so used to texting and e-mailing. They are losing their verbal skills completely.

Some of the numbers are astounding. In October of 2012, Facebook announced that it had reached one billion members—three times the number of people in the entire United States and nearly one in every seven people on the planet. A Pew Internet study in 2012 reported that cell phone owners age eighteen to twenty-four in the United States exchange 3,200 text messages per month, about 110 per day. If a person wakes up at seven in the morning and goes to bed at eleven at night, that means they're sending or receiving a text message every eight and a half minutes or so—and that's only text messaging. Twitter is now reporting it handles 400 million Tweets per day, and a billion every two and a half days.

What do people do? They use it as an outlet for frustration. A player is unhappy with something in a game and gets on Twitter on the bus afterward and lashes out. Someone is angry with a boss or coworker and gets onto Facebook to vent. Someone gets a promotion—or gets passed over—and has to get on social media to shout it to the world; but as with coaches, what good is this doing them? If you're in a crisis and updating everyone on Twitter, you're only giving people something they can use against you. Even worse, you're spending time posting on social media that you could be using to work, to be more productive, to work your way into a better situation.

Perhaps even worse, you're turning people off. We talk a lot to our players about turning people on with our behavior, being engaging with people and having them walk away with a positive feeling, not turning people off. One of the biggest turnoffs today is when people go out to dinner or have meetings and take out their phones right in the middle of it. If you can't give your undivided attention to the people you're with, they get upset.

My rule with players is the same as it is with my children: If we are having a team or family event, even just dinner, and the phone goes off, I take it away for the night. I don't use a phone during those times either. Those are important times that require and deserve our undivided attention. I understand this is against the norm in our society today. I was once part of that norm. I did the same thing until I caught myself and realized it was making demands on my focus, so I don't do it anymore. I was succumbing to the culture, and I told myself I wouldn't do it any longer. In the past year, I have stopped taking my phone into restaurants for dinner. My wife says, take it, what if the kids call. I say, if they need us, they'll find us. We didn't have cell phones for years and it worked all right. Why people think they have to answer a meaningless text or e-mail while they're in the company of others is one of the strangest phenomena I've witnessed. It takes away from their ability to communicate, a vital element to success.

FOCUSING ON THE CRAP

Even more dangerous than losing communication skills is losing the ability to think, and studies are beginning to show that the more time we spend online, the more it can literally rewire our brains to think in new ways— and not for the better. I talked in our last chapter about Russ Smith and his improved focus late in the season. Let's go back to his lack of focus for his early career at Louisville. Russ is the best on our team, nobody touches him, at the NBA Xbox games. He kills everyone. But he was, for the longest time, the most distracted guy in practice I know. He could not sit still, could not pay attention to what was going on offensively and defensively. The guys I've coached in the last five to seven years could not sit down for forty minutes without checking their phone or computer and iPad.

This isn't just an anecdotal story. Studies bear out that spending more time on the Web or with games creates a need in our minds for even more similar stimulation, and conditions us against focusing on tasks for longer periods of time. Beyond that, it actually physically changes our brains. A study done in China performed MRIs on the brains of eighteen college students who spent ten hours a day online. Compared with a group that spent two hours a day or less online, the heavy Web users had less gray matter—the part of the brain used for thinking.

Nicholas Carr says in his book, "The Net seizes our attention only to scatter it. We focus intensively on the medium itself, on the flickering screen, but we're distracted by the medium's rapid-fire delivery of competing messages and stimuli." In an interview with Carr, neuroscientist Michael Merzenich said that as we multitask online, "We are training our brains to pay attention to the crap."

That's a good description of what we find. For every person who enjoys reading compliments or validation through social media, there is one who sees comments online and comes away irritated or negative. Read the wrong thing someone has said and it can eat at you all day—and who has time to devote the mental and emotional energy to that? Realize the cost to yourself of some of these distractions.

Google, in fact, counts on us becoming distracted from our original Web searches by clicking on other subjects. That's how it makes money. It's in the distraction business. "The more we use the Web," Carr says, "the more we train our brains to be distracted."

Add the effect of this on young people, who are exposed to this type of stimulus at an early age and often know nothing else, and you have a crisis of critical thinking ability—or the lack of it. David Levy, a professor with the Information School at the University of Washington, calls it "popcorn brain." We get so used to the constant popping of new information online that our minds are less fit for life in the real world, where the information "pops" more slowly.

I can't stress this enough, for parents or others taking care of children who are reading this. One of the most important things, I think, for parents to do is this: When children come home from school and have to do their homework, remove all electronics from the environment. Kids must learn not only to get the job done with their homework, but they have to learn how to focus. I mentioned earlier in this chapter that in France, attention deficit diagnoses are not as prevalent as they are in other developed nations. One reason for this could be child rearing. According to the recent book *Bringing up Bébé,* by Pamela Druckerman, French parents provide their children with a well-defined cadre, a French word meaning "structure." Mealtimes are strictly scheduled. French children are trained to be patient. Parents don't scurry to respond immediately to every request their child makes.

Linda Stone worked for years as an executive at Apple and then at Microsoft Research in the 1980s and 1990s. She coined the term "continuous partial attention" to describe our current state of focus, or lack of it. We're always focused on everything without really focusing on anything. Stone was interviewed by *The Atlantic* in its June 2013 issue and said this:

"We learn by imitation, from the very start. That's how we're wired. . . . Professors at the University of Washington I-Labs show babies at 42 minutes old, imitating adults. The adult sticks his tongue out. The baby sticks his tongue out, mirroring the adult's behavior. Children are also cued by where a parent focuses attention. The child's gaze follows the mother's gaze. Not long ago, I had brunch with friends who are doctors, and both of them were on call. They were constantly pulling out their smartphones. The focus of their 1-year-old turned to the smartphone: Mommy's got it, Daddy's got it. I want it.

"We may think that kids have a natural fascination with phones. Really, children have a fascination with whatever Mom and Dad find fascinating."

As someone who works professionally with young people after all these habits have been formed, I can tell you that it is one major difference between college-age people today and those twenty years ago. The real fallout, however, is being seen by people in the workplace and the managers and companies who employ them.

Not only arc people wasting time by surfing the Net, but even the demands of work-related e-mails or electronic messages are slowing them down. If, as the Harvard study suggests, every interruption slows you down as much as 25 percent on the task you were originally working on, how much slower are you working if you are stopping to respond to just four e-mails an hour?

Joanne Cantor, director for the Center for Communication Research at the University of Wisconsin-Madison, wrote a book titled *Conquer CyberOverload*. She said, "What the managers don't understand is that they are asking employees to lower their intelligence levels. They're asking them to dim their bulbs. When you're constantly being interrupted your brain is not operating at its full capacity."

I'm not a Luddite. I understand we live in a technological world. It's wonderful in many ways, but each of us needs to make a serious assessment of whether we are using technology to become more effective, or allowing it to make us more distracted and less effective.

RECLAIMING YOUR FOCUS

As you can see, this technological overload is a formidable obstacle to focus. It feeds into the way our brains are already wired for distraction, then presses down the gas and drives us full-speed away from the things we need to be concentrating on. So how can it be combated? For Russ Smith, getting more interested in watching scouting video than in playing video games was the start of a major transformation. A simple shift can pay big dividends. The first step is to realize how much time you are spending online or on other means of technological distraction. Particularly with football teams, one thing coaches do is self-scout. They watch film of their own teams to determine their own tendencies, to try to pick up on trends opposing coaches may be seeing. In this instance, paying attention to how much time a day you spend online, and how much time you spend online not accomplishing anything, is a first start to attacking the problem.

Increasingly, businesses are recommending designated time periods for answering e-mails and text messages, or corresponding in other ways online. Set aside fifteen to twenty minutes to answer messages, then stop and don't do it again until the next session. This allows you to avoid the constant interruptions of e-mails landing in your inbox.

For those whose work is on the Web, or on computer screens, a number of software developers have come up with programs that will block the Web for a designated time. Many writers report that they turn their Internet off at the source, their modem, before sitting down to write. Others, as famous as Larry McMurtry and Woody Allen, still use manual typewriters to compose their books and scripts, because computers and word processors pose too many potential distractions.

Some psychologists suggest physically getting away from the computer to look out the window or to take a short walk. Time online speeds your brain up, and you need it to slow down at times to focus and concentrate better.

Finally, you cannot allow online outlets to become an escape. It's easy, when there's daunting work to be done, jobs to be pursued, projects to be completed, to enter the world of social media and to paint yourself however you want to be, to hear from friends who are all too eager to waste time with you. It even can alter your view of yourself. Some people begin to believe that they are this persona they create through their Facebook posts and pictures thrown online, and they lose a realistic view of themselves. I can tell when my players are losing focus. I'll see how they walk and talk. They'll be wearing fake glasses with clear lenses. Not seeing yourself realistically is an obstacle to focus. Social media is a haven for those who don't want to look at themselves realistically.

Recently, Dallas Cowboy defensive back Orlando Scandrick appeared on the show *Million Dollar Listing,* a program on the Bravo cable television network in which real estate brokers show high-priced homes to wealthy clients. In Scandrick's case, the agent was taking him through a $4 million home, room by room, but the rookie had interest in only one thing—the smartphone in his hands. The agent described each room and tried to point out features to Scandrick, but the player seemed unable to pull himself away from the phone. Finally the player said, "You know, I can't do this. Just get with my business advisor and he'll find something." Scandrick was making probably the biggest investment of his life, but he couldn't be bothered to pay attention because he was too wrapped up in whatever was going on in his Twitter and text world. That's an extreme case, but on a smaller scale many people every day are turning their attention from those things that could affect their future or improve their lives, work, and careers, toward a technological time machine that claims time but never gives it back.

I know this chapter will hit home for many. Before you dismiss what I'm saying, however, make sure you look realistically at the role technology is playing in your life. Compile a stat sheet of your own online life, how much of your time and focus is going into that. I am convinced that those who exercise good judgment concerning technology will have a significant professional edge in the coming years. Used as a tool, it can help you greatly. Allow it to work its distracting power on you, and you'll always find focus elusive, and success very difficult. No coach or player would pause during a game to send a Tweet or stop to see what people were saying about him on social media. With our program, I take it a step further. During the season, players are not allowed to Tweet, not even on days off or nongame days. Simply put, it is too big a distraction from all they have going on with basketball and school. It may seem extreme, but it's hard to argue with the results. Our team posted the highest grade point average in the program's history in the same season it won an NCAA championship. During the season, we can't afford to let some of today's technology rob us of our time. We're not alone. If you are in season in your life or career, you can't afford to take too many technological timeouts.

4

When Adversity Strikes

For over thirty years I have preached one strong constant to my players—that when you tell the truth your problems become part of your past, but when you lie they become part of your future. That was never more evident than in a vicious extortion ordeal that I experienced, or in the difficult trial and testimony I had to endure as a result of it. In this chapter, I will share how I handled those things, how I navigated that time, and emerged with my life intact. This is a difficult chapter to write, because it deals with some agonizing times in my life. I write it knowing that there are many people who will open this book and seek out these pages first. That's how life is today. I write it not to offer explanation, but because it was a chapter in my life and not to write it would be wrong. More than that, however, I write it because it may be of some use. Some of the things I share with you here, in fact, may be among the most useful things you encounter in these pages.

I'm not going to recount the actions that got me into that situation. I placed my hand on a Bible, went under oath, and spent hours testifying in excruciating detail. When it comes to telling my side of that particular story, it's been told. I will say that how it happened, how I got into that situation, I still don't completely understand. I'm not sure I ever will. Here I was, a married man with a high-profile job, interacting with the wrong kind of person. It was a personal and moral failure. I should not have been within a hundred yards of that situation. There are only so many ways I can say that I made a mistake, and I let people down. I was wrong.

I am not minimizing those actions. But the subject here, handling adversity and getting through difficult times, is less about how we get into difficult situations than how we get through them. Whether we bring them on ourselves or they are forced upon us, difficult times come, and it is what we do once they have arrived that is important. Here I was, having made a terrible mistake, and I knew that it sat like a powder keg under my life and my family. More than anything, I wanted it not to blow up. I knew the consequences of it going public. I knew, or thought I knew, what it would put my family through, not to mention my university and myself. I did not want the truth out there. But the truth was the only road out. I knew it was going to hurt many people, and for a long time. But the truth was what was called for. There was no other way.

I've been through some difficult times in my life. I don't know that I've done anything more difficult than telling the truth to my wife, Joanne, and my family. My pain during that time was severe. There may be no worse feeling than being the source of immense pain to people you love. The guilt involved, along with having to watch them suffer the consequences of your action, only magnifies your own pain. But as bad as I felt, I could tell that they were hurting more. Not only were they disappointed, angry, and hurt by my actions, but they had to deal with watching someone they love and respect go through this very public spectacle, to reach rock bottom, in some ways. I wanted there to be something I could do to ease the pain that my family felt. But when you're the source of the pain, sometimes there's nothing you can do. Time and forgiveness are the only things that can heal such a situation, and neither of those will be rushed. They come on their own timetable. In a mess of this magnitude, you pay day by day.

Part of that payment is being open with all of the parties involved. For me that began at home, but it quickly extended to my employers at the University of Louisville, people within my program, and finally the media and fans. It started with Tom Jurich, my boss and vice president for athletics at Louisville. I went to him and explained everything, leaving nothing out. He listened to me, nodding, asking questions here and there, including some hard questions. It was a difficult conversation to have, because I knew that I was putting both him and the university in a terrible situation. After telling Tom everything, I told him right up front, "If it will make it easier on you for me to step down, I will." He did not hesitate before answering, "As long as I am athletic director, that will never happen." As a trusted friend, Tom was able to help me. When the time came to meet with university officials and attorneys, Tom came in with me, and my wife was nearby in case they wanted to question her. Again, I explained the situation and answered their questions. After I finished, there was some talk by university lawyers that maybe I should take a leave of absence for family purposes, and for them to look at the matter more closely. They were still debating it when Tom spoke up, and said that if I were off the job for even one day, they would have the added task of looking for a new athletic director. I stayed on the job. Looking back, staying on the job was an important factor not only in my getting through the whole experience, but also in building the success we would eventually recapture.

You learn a lot of things during an ordeal like that.

You learn about yourself and what you can take. You find out about your capacity to disappoint people and how much your actions can hurt them. You learn how much stress your mind and body can endure. And you find out who your true friends are.

It didn't take this experience for me to find out who my friends were, but it certainly confirmed it, in case there was ever any reason to wonder. You'll also learn about your capacity for gratitude, because the friends who stand by you and help you when times are that tough are some of the greatest gifts in all of life. Ralph Willard has been one of my closest friends for decades. He was coaching at his alma mater, Holy Cross, and he loved coaching there. He had been a three-time conference coach of the year, a national coach of the year finalist, and had one of his best teams coming back. It was going to be a season for which he had been building. And when my crisis hit, he just walked away. He resigned and came to Louisville because he felt he needed to be here beside me. It was the greatest gift of friendship I'd ever witnessed, and certainly ever received. Ralph went through every difficult moment with me. He supported me, worked long hours, did a phenomenal coaching job with our guys, and was with me for every step. He was by my side the day I told my son Richard, an assistant coach for us, what had transpired. It was an act of friendship vast enough for a lifetime. And there were others, which you'll read about in the coming pages.

One thing you will encounter if you find yourself in such a crucible, whether of your own making or not, is that there will be advice on all sides. I'm used to receiving a lot of input from assistant coaches, but this was something different entirely. The number of opinions on what I needed to do or how I should handle things was both fascinating and exasperating. The lawyers had one kind of advice. The FBI had another. Then there were friends, family, and we even consulted some public relations firms. We spoke to Ari Fleischer, a former White House press secretary. But in the end, I decided against bringing in any advisor. I realized I would have to make the ultimate decisions myself. There were so many differences of opinion that I was going to be deciding myself, anyway. All of that input, however, did serve a valuable purpose.

Another lesson: When you are strapped in to take a lie detector test, your life changes in front of you. I was on the road when my attorney, Steve Pence, called and said that this woman was making all kinds of accusations on ESPN. He told me, "We know that you're telling the truth, but would you take a lie detector test?" I was back on a plane to Louisville immediately. I told Steve to get the best person in the country and he said he already had the guy. Carl Christiansen is a former

FBI special agent who travels around the country instructing on how to administer polygraph tests. He was living in nearby Simpsonville, Kentucky, and was able to come in and administer the test to me. I passed.

But even Carl had an opinion on what I should do. He told me to urge the FBI to settle, to offer her some kind of deal. "Don't get on that witness stand," he told me. "When you get up there, her lawyer will humiliate you. I've been in many courtrooms and have seen it happen. I always cringe. You are better off staying off that witness stand, no matter what."

Those words echoed in my mind for a long time. But the FBI had another opinion. They wanted me to cooperate with their prosecution. They told me that this woman didn't want a plea deal, that this situation had happened before with other men, and that it would not stop unless I went through with this. I told them that was easy for them to say. For them, this was a potential victory in a big case. That was their game. But for me, I'd be on the stand alone, for everybody to see with nowhere to hide in an excruciating situation.

This is where Whitey Moynihan entered the discussion. A close friend of Ralph Willard's and mine, Whitey is an international covert specialist. That's the best way I can describe his job without going into more detail than I should. Like everyone else, Whitey had an opinion. He said, "It's time for you to eat your ten tons of crap." Except he didn't say "crap." He told me to fight for my family. "Eat crap for a long time," he told me repeatedly. "This is just something you're going to have to go through."

That wasn't exactly what I wanted to hear. I argued that it would hurt my family and me. I argued that would humiliate my family and me. He agreed. "Yes, it will," he said. "But the hurt will go away with honesty. The hurt will go away with telling the truth."

He was right. I can tell you today that the hurt has subsided. Now, what happened will never go away. My actions cannot be erased. This situation will always be a footnote on my story in certain situations. But the more truth you tell, the more you shrink the problem down in size, and the more it shrinks in your mind.

You might not have to climb onto that witness stand. You might not have to be strapped into that polygraph chair. But you will encounter circumstances and difficult situations that require you to make a decision on the truth. The interesting lesson from my situation was that there was no way out but the truth. The only alternative was losing everything I had worked so hard to build, and letting down the people I love even more. The truth was the only way. Period. The slightest little cover-up, the smallest lie or bending of the truth, will cost you dearly.

We all fear telling the truth at times. We tell

ourselves that a lie would help ease the pain for others, and minimize the consequences for ourselves. I told myself that. I never wanted any of this to see the light of day. Even once the truth is told, when you return home and look in the mirror, the feeling of personal disgust doesn't disappear overnight. What the truth does, however, is create a path to solutions.

In looking at people who have been cut down by scandal, I think about Eliot Spitzer in politics, or more recently Arkansas football coach Bobby Petrino or Congressman Anthony Weiner, who lost their careers, at least for a time, to scandal. With them and others in similar situations, there is one constant. They did not tell the truth. Coach Petrino came out in a press conference and didn't disclose the details of his motorcycle accident. Better to say nothing than to go public with a story that was not the truth. Weiner originally said his improper conduct on Twitter was a prank someone was playing on him. These only compounded already ugly truths.

Show me someone who has been cut down by events—either self-inflicted or from outside influences—and I'll show you someone who could not find the strength to at long last tell the truth. That is what people are looking for from people in tough situations. On the flip side, show me someone who has weathered those crises and gone on to prosper, and you will find at some point they had to level with themselves, their families, their coworkers or companies, and in some cases, the public. Bobby Petrino lost his job at Arkansas, but during the offseason sat down with ESPN and endured an interview that I know was personally painful for him. To admit your wrongdoing, to lay it out publicly, is a difficult thing. But having done that, Bobby freed himself to move forward. Once he did that, his mistakes were part of his past, and he was able to begin building his future, which he now is doing right down the road at Western Kentucky University.

I wish I could tell you that after all my dread of getting up on the witness stand, the experience wasn't as bad as I feared it would be. I'd like to be able to tell you that my absolute terror at the prospect was worse than the reality of going through it. I can't tell you that. As much as I feared this time on the stand, the actual experience was worse.

Confession may be good for the soul, but it also can be hell on it. It was an ordeal. To tell the most intimate truth on the most public stage, the media reporting every detail, I wouldn't wish on anyone. I didn't want it for myself. It came to a point on the stand, with the public defender aggressively cross-examining me, where I wanted to take him outside and whip his ass. But Carl had told me ahead of time, that's his job, don't make it personal. And Whitey convinced me, "You have to go through this, because it's your punishment for screwing up. Think of it that way. Not only are you doing the right thing by doing this, but it's your punishment. And when you go on the road, that's your punishment, too." Whitey convinced me that it was basic penance, and that I was going to have to go through it, there was no way around it. Sometimes it is as simple as that. You sow with your actions, you reap the consequences.

At every step, Whitey told me exactly what was going on and what was going to happen next, and the more he talked the more afraid and nervous I became. But I needed to know the truth and how to deal with it. Unsettling as it was, it still was preferable to being hit with the unknown. In difficult times, fear can make us retreat into a shell, to ignore the consequences that are coming, as sure as the sunrise. But it's always better to know what is going to be there when the light of day comes. Value those people who are willing to give you the hard truth during those dark nights of the soul. And don't shy away from hearing it in times of crisis. It will prepare you for the hard work of healing.

Another interesting thing happened during my most difficult times. Bob Russell, the gifted preacher who helped build a congregation of a hundred or so people in Louisville into one of more than 20,000—one of the nation's largest churches—at Southeast Christian Church, called me one day and wanted to see me. He came to my office and said, "You don't know me very well, I've prayed with your team a couple of times before games, but I had somebody tell me I needed to come see you, that you needed a friend right now, maybe someone to be with."

I asked him, "Who was that, Bob?"

He answered, "The Lord."

That took me aback. I had never had someone say that the Lord had sent him to me. But we sat and talked. And then he talked to my wife, with me, on two occasions. Then we started meeting regularly.

He asked me how much I knew about the Bible, and I said, well, eight years of Catholic school, four years of high school, countless church services, but I really didn't give it deep thought. I listened in church, but really didn't put much interpretation into the meaning of it. He said, "Would you like to find out more about it?" At the time, I said yes, but didn't know I truly meant it, because of so many things that were going on in my life. It seemed like a good thing to do, but I did not know what to expect. I can tell you now, however, that I wound up enjoying and appreciating those times of reading the Bible and discussing it with Bob as much as anything I did during those difficult times, because he was able to share so much insight, and to give such a human touch to all of these things that were going on centuries ago.

Just like reading a great book, sitting down and looking at the Bible and the interpretations and insight that Bob had was something I found fascinating. You get the perspective that human beings are much the same today as they were thousands of years ago, struggling with the same trials and temptations. At some point, Bob asked if I minded having someone join us, and he invited David Novak, the CEO of Yum! Brands; David is known as one of the top CEOs in the world. Because of our time in Bible study, I developed a strong friendship and great respect for David. We truly enjoyed discussing the applications and interpretations of everything we were reading. And Bob always kept in touch with me throughout the season. When he could hear on TV or radio broadcasts that I was taking a lot of heat on the road, he would text me, "How you doing? Great win. Did you turn the other cheek? Were you able to get through it?" And I would text back and we would talk about it. And he will still text me things from time to time.

The road was a difficult aspect in all of this. With the notoriety of my story, opposing fan bases were lying in wait. One surprising thing was that, with the exception of fans at West Virginia, which was the worst, the fans at Catholic schools were the hardest on me. The best? Surprisingly, because of the rivalry, fans at the University of Kentucky were the classiest to me. Their student section could have really buried me, but didn't.

All through that period, I kept saying the same thing over and over, "Win the game." When I would hear things. "Win the game." When the stories would come out. "Win the game." When someone would say something insulting. "Win the game." I was like a toy with a string in the back. (It gives me chills to think about it today. Those are the same words that Kevin Ware, with his broken bone having torn through his leg, kept repeating to our team on that sideline against Duke. A different kind of adversity, to be sure, but interesting that the mantra was the same.) I never considered myself a person who could turn the other cheek, and didn't know if I could do it. But Bob really convinced me of the importance of doing it, gave me biblical examples of it, and I was able to do it in most instances without any problem. Without him, I don't know if I could have turned the other cheek as often as I did.

For a renowned preacher like Bob Russell, and for a guy like David Novak, the CEO of the largest food company in the world, to care enough to sit down and open up with me is something I'll never forget as long as I live.

I didn't always turn the other cheek. When you feel you're being lied about and your character is being distorted, it's difficult to sit still. It's bad enough that you have brought this awful blot on your own character, but when you feel people are lying about it and giving a platform to put forth sheer falsehoods about you or your actions, it makes you very competitive in wanting to get your side of the story out there. And that's what I did. Months after the original story broke, local outlets began to air tapes with the same ludicrous allegations against me that, in the end, were proven to be nothing but illegal and false accusations aimed at extorting me. There was nothing new. Every bit of it had been printed in the news media already. Our sports information director, Kenny Klein, even told me one local television station cut into coverage of the death of Ted Kennedy with a story about me, because now there were allegations on tape, and I was disgusted. I was angry, and wanted to set the record straight. I called a press conference and said my piece. I wanted to get up and say, "These are lies you are putting on your airwaves," and I did. But nothing good came out of it. I accomplished nothing but looking angry on television. I was criticized for holding the press conference and I was criticized for what I said during the press conference. One thing that I came to realize is that in the midst of a bad situation, when something comes out and you want to answer it, don't answer it. Nothing good can come of it. If somebody needs to give an answer, let your attorney do it.

After the press conference was over and I saw the response, I told myself, "That's it. I'm only talking when I have to—no more press conferences, and I'm not discussing it anymore." Having gone through it, I'm convinced that's the best way to handle it.

These truths are easy to understand, but hard to practice. I see it with our players. I remember one night a player letting a female into our dormitory and breaking curfew. Security cameras caught his actions. When confronted, his response was almost laughable. He said he heard a knock at the outside door (which was physically impossible), then came down the steps and checked the girl's identification before letting her in the door. My look of disgust and disbelief gave away my feelings. I explained that if he had owned up to the truth, the punishment would've been physical training in the early morning hours. But now it would be worse. The lie would get worse as he watched more action on the surveillance tape. I tell our guys, when I was their age, there was no technology to tell if we sneaked out or broke curfew. But with technology today, you can't do anything without everybody finding out within minutes. If you're drinking alcohol, the public will know. If you're doing the wrong thing, the public will know. If you're doing the right thing, the public will know. Your life is an open book now if you play sports. And we give our players examples and talk about it and showcase it.

The truth, on the other hand, stimulates growth in relationships. It builds character in those who tell it. And most of all, the truth allows you to solve your problems, to manage your difficult times, and maneuver through all the roadblocks that stand in your way.

The major problem with lying is that it never stops. More lies will have to come to cover up the original lie. I could give a hundred experiences from players over my thirty-five years in coaching. The stories are always the same. That's why it's been such a blessing the past two years. The current group of players I coach understand the importance of telling the truth regardless of the ramifications. The truth allows them to move forward. They own up, pay the consequences, and their errors are learned and thus become part of their past. It's no different for anyone, the careers lost and lives destroyed span every field. If the original mistake doesn't ruin people, the cover-up finishes the job.

As I look back on my life of teaching players, so many lie to themselves to take the easy road. The simple question "Did you put in a hard day's work in the offseason to improve?" often gets the easy answer: "Yes, Coach." The truth always is revealed when the time for supervised workouts begins. The bigger problem is the lie to one's self. The best answer in such situations is: "It could always be better." Just as lying breeds more lies, telling the truth becomes a natural habit—and one of the best that can be formed. I've learned the easy way, from watching the consequences for players, and the hard way.

One of the toughest aspects of this kind of adversity is that you have to start by telling the truth to yourself. So many of us don't view ourselves realistically. We believe the lies we tell the world. The first person you have to be truthful with is yourself. If you are not, one personal failure can compound to every area of your life. It is well documented. To the outside world, to your boss and everyone else, telling the truth is not the most difficult thing. Accepting the truth for yourself, then telling the truth to your family, is the most difficult thing in the world, but it's the only way for forgiveness to take shape. As Bob Russell told me, it's not going to happen instantly. It could take months, even years. But you will be forgiven. And his main point to me was, in the end, the most important one you've got to make sure of—and you're going to think of your spouse right away—the most important one you're going to find is the Lord. You better make sure you're forgiven by him, first and foremost.

The other tough part of this kind of truth telling is that it is better for everyone involved if they hear it from you. For a short time before the news of all of this broke, I knew that this woman was going to the media all over town to try to tell her story. No one could find any evidence that any of the allegations were true, so no one ran a word about it. But the allegations were out there, and I knew it was only a matter of time until they became public. In this day and age, everything will become public. You can count on it. I had been talking to the FBI for some time once the extortion attempts began. My son Richard had already made the decision to leave to join Billy Donovan's staff at the University of Florida. When Eric Crawford, then with the *Courier-Journal,* called me to say he had heard that the allegations were around town, I knew that the awful time had come that I was going to have to speak about this. I was already prepared, as well as I believed I could be. I had already spoken to my family, to Tom Jurich, to my university bosses and attorneys and public relations staff. It was time. I released a statement, one that had been crafted in consultation with my attorney, saying that I was cooperating with the FBI, that many of the allegations against me were wrong and part of an extortion attempt against me, and that I would defend my character and fight for my family. Over time, I would have to disclose many more things that were painful and embarrassing. It was an action I had hoped I never would have to take, and one I tried to avoid. But it was, in the end, unavoidable, and when the time came, I felt it was important for me to say the first word publicly.

I'm not sharing these things as someone who has always had all the answers. I'm writing this knowing that I've made big mistakes. And when these truths were presented to me with the prospect of an extortion trial, a large part of me did not want to go ahead with the trial. I wanted anything but that. I wanted something that would make it all go away as quickly as it could. A trial would be painful, most of all for my family. And it would be humiliating and infuriating to take the witness stand and be grilled by a defense attorney. From the minute I embarked on that course, there were miserable days ahead for my family and me. My only escape was to work with my players and my team, and to talk with my friends. And my only way out was facing the truth.

Until you tell the truth, starting with the person in the mirror, nobody's forgiving you. Nobody. Not yourself, not your family, not your friends, until you own up to things as they truly stand.

Now I want to stop for a moment and talk to a special group of you out there—those who have endured tragedy in their lives. Not all adversity in life is self-induced. I have written about these things before, but in some ways I think they need to be revisited now more than ever. Tragedy is a part of all our lives now—real, genuine, heartbreaking tragedy—whether it hits us directly or we watch it from afar. There are images on television you cannot watch without tears. There is violence; the shootings at the elementary school in Newtown, Connecticut and the terrorist bombing at the finish line of the Boston Marathon are only the most recent examples. But such senseless events have happened in increasing number since the September 11, 2001, terrorist attacks: the Virginia Tech massacre, a pair of snipers in the Washington, D.C., area, a mass shooting in a Colorado movie theater, the headlines only grow worse. And when it isn't violence, it's natural disaster. Superstorm Sandy devastated parts of the Northeast. A tornado hit Moore, Oklahoma, with a direct hit on an elementary school. I pray that not many people reading these pages have been touched by this kind of sudden tragedy, but I know that many of you have. And certainly, many know that I have.

I lost an infant son, Daniel, to crib death. He was born prematurely and weighed only four pounds. There was a host of complications. He had a hole in his heart that would require surgery when he was strong enough. He had a space in his palate that made eating difficult. We were living in Providence, Rhode Island, where I was coach and Joanne was driving the hour and a half each way every day, spending twelve-hour days at the

Boston hospital where Daniel was being cared for, feeding him with a special nipple. Under her care and the doctors' care, he thrived. He grew enough to come home until the time came for his heart surgery. Doctors told her it would be good for her to get away when our Providence team was playing in the Big East Tournament, which was two and a half hours away in New York City. Daniel and his three older brothers were left for the weekend with the nanny.

But on a jubilant bus ride back from New York, after the Big East Tournament, a state trooper pulled our bus over to the side of the road. I thought he was just there to tell us where we'd be playing in the NCAA Tournament. Instead, he said I needed to come with him. They took me to a phone booth and put me on the line with the hospital in Providence. I asked to know what was wrong and they said they would rather tell me in person. I demanded that they tell me right then, and Dr. Joe Flynn, crying, told me that Daniel had died. For anyone who has ever experienced that moment, you know that you are never the same person again, as long as you live. I could not bring myself to say the words. I had to lean down and whisper to Joanne. She collapsed, unconscious, in my arms, right on that Rhode Island roadside. The sight of the tiny casket, the chilling numbness of the coming weeks and months, they never completely leave you.

In the aftermath of that, I wanted to stop coaching, to be with Joanne and my boys. But she wouldn't let me. She told me I had to go on. And I did. I have learned over the course of my life that I was the lucky one. I could walk into the gym and put my mind on getting to work. I could focus on the step-by-step routine of the day, if only for a little while. Even the night Daniel died, when I got home, I could not sleep. I put on game tapes and watched them over and over. Others may tell you differently about coping with tragedy and adversity. I can tell you, in many ways, your work and your daily purposeful activity is your therapy. Our first NCAA Tournament game was just two days after the funeral, in Birmingham, Alabama. The NCAA allowed me to send Stu Jackson to the mandatory press conferences to represent our team. They told reporters that there would be no questions about my son. Joanne did not come to Birmingham, but I told her after coming home that if she did not come to Louisville, for the next round of the regionals, I wasn't going either. So she came, and after the games we retreated to the hotel into our own world. People have described that amazing Final Four run with Providence in 1987 as magical, and over the years, I've come to realize that it was incredibly special. Those players and coaches who surrounded me have become friends for life. I saw them at our twenty-fifth reunion of that Final Four and we laughed and cried together.

What I learned through that is that we are called upon to move on with life. We have no choice but to move forward. The thing to which we have devoted our lives is the thing that will help us weather what life brings us. I would use that knowledge again after September 11. Billy Minardi, my wife's younger brother, was my best friend in life. He died on the 105th floor of the North Tower of the World Trade Center. It came just months after Don Vogt, the husband of my wife's sister, had been struck and killed by a taxi in New York City. I don't know how long I lived in shock after those events. My life, again, and Joanne's life, changed forever. Hardly a day goes by that I don't miss Billy at some point, and during our national championship run in 2013, I thought of him even more. But his wife and children live in Louisville near us now. And I draw strength from family and from our team, which is a second family. There was a time after Billy's death that the wind was taken from my sails. Basketball did not seem as important to me as it once did, and it never would. There was bitterness and anger to deal with. I'm sure I didn't deal with all those things the right way. Moving on is not a fast process. It takes years. But the daily requirement of showing up for life, facing the days and making the most of them never stops. And it is in fulfilling those tasks that we begin our road back. There's no easy answer. There's no easy process.

There is a homeless shelter in Owensboro, Kentucky, named after Daniel. Our players' dormitory at Louisville, and one tournament or special game per year is played in Billy's honor and is named for him. If the adversity you are facing today involves the blows that tragedy can level in your life through no fault of your own, the difficult road back is no less rooted in the truth for you than for anyone else facing difficulty. Life won't stop. And your charge is to live it as well as you can live it, and to achieve those things you believe you are here to achieve. Keep going. If there are good things around the corner, we cannot experience them unless we get there. There is no easy answer. There's no easy process.

I only share these things for the same reason I talk about my experience in bringing adversity on myself, and that's to show that there can be something good on the other side. I could make a list; I can try to share my truths; I can hazard some advice, but in the end the best thing I can show you is my life. The pieces can be put back together, no matter how they get broken, whether through blind misfortune or our own actions.

In the end, there will be times in life when you tell the truth that you will eat crow, or as my friend Whitey would say, eat your ten tons of crap. There will be times when you must swallow your own grief and bitterness and will yourself forward. Whatever the consequences are, you've got to get through them. And whatever the consequences are, hard as it is to see and believe when you're going through it, once you get through them, these difficult times will be part of your past and not your future.

You may never face a public trial, but most of us face difficult times. And in those, our road map out is to tell the truth, seek valued friendships, maintain a focus on work and life, and take spiritual stock of ourselves. The road of deception and cover-ups leads to a fall. Only the truth can return us to a path of success and happiness.

I don't want to wrap this up with too nice a ribbon. I don't want to take the Pollyanna approach that all adversity can be peeled back to reveal a happy ending. I can only offer myself as proof that sometimes it does. And I can only give you the exhortation that the only way you will ever find out if it will for you is to keep pushing ahead. You cannot allow difficult times to swallow up your life. You must find a way to keep going, to keep doing those things you do well. They are your source of positive energy in your life, when you are surrounded by negative events.

For four chapters now, we have talked about some

fundamentals of dealing with difficult times. We have talked about attitude (humility) and approach (focus). We took a timeout to deal with the trap of technology, and the immediate challenge of adversity when it strikes in its various and darkest forms. Now we will approach an important step in not only dealing with difficult times, but in bringing out your best in such a way that you can find your best days ever.

5

The One-Day Contract

In a career as long as mine has been, as you might imagine, I've signed many contracts. In this chapter, I'll tell you about one of the most important. I'm not talking about the most recent contract I signed, one that will keep me working as University of Louisville basketball coach until age seventy, if I'm fortunate enough to last that long. I'm not talking about the biggest contract I ever signed, to become president and head coach of the Boston Celtics. The contract I want to talk about in this chapter is one I make every day with myself.

Sitting with my brother-in-law Billy Minardi years ago along with a group of Wall Street brokers after a New York Knicks game, we were talking about one of the Knicks who signed a long-term contract and was playing with no urgency and no hustle, because he was very content with his long, secure deal. I said, "That's our biggest mistake in sports. Guys play their best in the last year of their contracts." Their response to me is what stimulated my mind for the title of this chapter. They said, "Here on Wall Street, we don't have one-year contracts or multiyear contracts. We are only as good as our last trade. One severe case in poor judgment can land us in the unemployment office." It stands to reason, if you're always at your best toward the end of your contract, why not try to create a situation where you can capture that mentality all the time?

It really hit home for me three years ago, after a first-round loss to Morehead State in the NCAA Tournament, when I seriously pondered retirement for the first time. I had friends who had retired and enjoyed it. I had done some work with TBS and CBS during the NCAA Tournament and I've always enjoyed that. An agent told me he could land me a lucrative offer as an analyst. But my wife convinced me that I'd drive myself crazy if I weren't coaching, and she's right. I realize now that I need the game too much. So over the past three years, a switch has flipped on for me. I have become more focused on making the most of the present than I ever have been, and more determined not to get caught up in all the superficial distractions. Even when we lost in the first round to Morehead State, I realized I had a great group of guys and I really enjoyed working with them. I resolved simply to enjoy coaching, to stop agonizing over things that did not matter, and most of all to play out the terms for the rest of my career in a series of one-day contracts. Sometimes, I admit that I'll finish a day and wonder whether even I would pick up my own option. But most days since adopting this philosophy I can honestly tell you I've coached as if the next day's contract depended on it. You won't always perform at your optimum, but you always can perform with the effort and mentality that a one-day contract would evoke, and that will certainly get the most out of your abilities.

The benefits can be immense. Ask yourself this question: Whatever your job is, whatever you're working at right now, how would life be different if you were on a one-day contract? How might your approach change if this afternoon after you finished work, a supervisor would make the call on whether to retain you for another day or let you go?

How would that affect your mind-set? My guess is you'd be tremendously organized, at least for that one day. Every minute of that day would be directly devoted to trying to maximize your effort. Wanting it now is fine, but sometimes people focus too much on the "wanting" and not on the "now." The one-day contract eliminates that. With a one-day contract, you're busting it until the final buzzer.

Look at underperforming NBA teams. Can you

imagine how they would perform if everyone were under a one-day contract? In college sports, we have scholarships that are one-year renewable. Sometimes I wish they were one-day renewable. It would solve the problems of some players. Some might think it would be stressful, but on the contrary, it would be an incredible motivator. (All right, I'm not seriously proposing that the NCAA do that, only wishing that many players would adopt that mind-set.) When you adopt a one-day contract mentality, it becomes less about what you are paid or what happened in the past than it is about what you can do today, and how you can make the most of what time you have.

The one-day contract is not unheard of in sports. Many times, an athlete ready to retire will sign a one-day contract with an organization so that he can retire as a member of that team. In short, athletes sign a one-day contract to finish their careers in the place they want to finish. For the rest of us, the one-day contract can result in the same outcome. It's a tool that can help up us finish the way we want to by reaching the goals we set. It's a mind-set, a way of looking at our lives and vocations that keeps our focus where it belongs and our effort at a high level. Knowing what we want to do isn't a problem for most of us. Coming up with a disciplined routine to get there is very difficult.

Every New Year's Day, millions of Americans set out with at least one new goal. We call them resolutions, and the implication is that they are things we will treat with resolve and determination. But *Forbes* magazine reported in January of 2013 that only 8 percent of the resolutions we make are accomplished over one year's time. According to a study by Franklin-Covey planning experts, a third of New Year's resolutions are broken by the end of January. What happens to the rest? You probably have experienced some of these things. People burn out on their goals, or they never get started, or they get discouraged, and regardless of what happens, they quit. If you hope to benefit from a one-day contract mentality, you must first address some of these things before you sign. In fact, you need to make three promises to yourself: You will not quit, you will not procrastinate, and you will not allow discouragement to sideline you. Let's look at these three important issues first, starting with procrastination, lest anyone be tempted to put off reading about it.

DON'T PROCRASTINATE

Procrastination may be the most dangerous habit keeping people from the lives they want to lead. One significant reason that we won a national championship in 2013 is that at no point did we procrastinate as a coaching staff, and our players did a good job of taking care of matters immediately. When I had the idea of moving Kevin Ware from shooting guard to point guard, we acted on it immediately. It turned out to be one of the most important moves we could have made. Sure, when you make a successful move, you always wish you had done it sooner. But in this case, and in others, we did not wait to act on ideas that we had.

A person on a one-day contract cannot afford to give in to procrastination. It takes away from all goal-oriented people. If you have a goal, immediately you must challenge yourself to come up with the plan of attack. You think about it in a twenty-four-hour span, and then you come up with your plan. And then along the way, you alter your path as you need to, because obstacles and detours do come up and impede you from going the direction you want to go. Whether it's the stock market and suddenly a foreign nation has a crisis that affects your ability to do what you want, or you're an oil and gas company and there's a spill somewhere, something always happens in the world of sports and business, and that's when you redirect, as we did with our basketball team, restating our goals after a rough stretch in which we lost four out of seven games.

It is vitally important, in basketball and business, that when you have an idea, you not just let it sit. I have note cards that I carry everywhere I go. All day long, when I get an idea or have a thought, I write it down. If I see something while watching a game or hear something someone says I put it down on the note card, then try to make that thought better or that play better as I carry it around with me. It's crucial in the competitive industry I'm in that I write every single thing down. After that, it's just as important to enhance the thoughts and ideas that move you enough to get onto your notecard or notebook. Don't let these things that come to you subside and pass away. Some of those things might be among your most valuable ideas.

In my case, it has become such a habit that to put something off is now against my nature. Some might think at times I act too quickly, but I have learned through long experience in my profession when to move quickly and when to give it time. For many people, however, procrastination ranks in the top five of their RPIs—Reaching-Potential Impediments. It's one of the great obstacles. *Psychology Today* estimates that 20 percent of people chronically avoid difficult tasks and deliberately seek distractions or excuses to keep from tackling them. The problem is as old as man. There's been a certain fascination with Leonardo da Vinci in recent years. He is considered one of the great painters in history and perhaps the most widely talented and brilliant man who ever lived, and two of his works, *Mona Lisa* and *The Last Supper*, are among the most reproduced in the history of mankind. In addition to his contributions in art, his notebooks left behind discoveries, ideas, and inventions that were centuries ahead of their time. His place in history is rock solid. But Leonardo died with regrets. He was, some people think because of his diverse talents and interests, a great procrastinator. He was easily distracted. He only finished *The Last Supper* when his patron threatened to stop paying him. He is said to have spent countless hours doodling into notebooks without finishing threads of thought. He had the advantage that his doodling was genius. Still, he died with regret. His last words were, "I have offended God and mankind because my work did not reach the quality it should have." Of course, we know from historical context that his work certainly lived on and left its mark. But the regret he died with, even a person of his talent and accomplishment, shows us the toll that procrastination can take. Every year, I have players return to practice at the start of school having put off doing all summer those things that they knew they needed to do to get better. People on a one-day contract enter the day, or enter their office or place of work, knowing precisely what things they will do that day.

So many times, players will enter the offseason with the plan of working on their game, strengthening certain aspects that coaches have suggested they work on, only to come back in the fall having made little progress. This was the case with one of our most talented players, Chane Behanan, before the 2012–13 season. He didn't have a productive summer, and as a result his season was not as productive as he had hoped it would be. At one point, Chane was thinking that he might have a chance to consider the NBA Draft after his sophomore season, but he hit a slump. Chane is a player with a great many distractions, and that can lead to not having a sense of urgency. Chane also is a player with a strong passion for the game and the highest of motivations for success—to provide a new life for his family after growing up in very rough circumstances in Cincinnati. For Chane, it was a procrastinating type of season. There were times when many were asking, "What is he waiting for?" But when the Final Four came around, there was no more waiting for Chane. When crunch time got to its most pressure-packed, Chane was the best he has been in his career. Look at these stats. In the second half of our semifinal win over Wichita State and the second half of our title game win over Michigan, Chane had a combined twenty-one points and seventeen rebounds. That's as big-time a stat line against the best competition in college basketball as any frontcourt player in the game could post. Yet it took until that stage and that time to see the Chane Behanan we had all wanted to see. In the locker room after the Wichita State game, Kevin Ware said of Behanan, "'Bout time Chane played." Across the way, Chane said, "Yeah, he's probably right." We're hoping that Chane won't put off becoming the player he is capable of being any longer.

If he'll sign a one-day contract, he can be one of the premier players in the nation.

You need to remember, procrastinating isn't just putting something off. It also can be doing something other than what you mean to be doing. It's going to the movies instead of going to work out. The great writer Victor Hugo would sometimes have his servant lock him in his house and take away all his clothes so he would have no other option but to stay in there and write. (Full disclosure: This entire book was written while fully clothed!) That's an example of how dangerous a trap he viewed distraction and procrastination to be, and how committed Hugo was to avoiding it. We talked about the distractions of technology, but any manner of distraction can be used to procrastinate. You can be perfectly busy at your desk, but still procrastinating. In his excellent book on the subject, *The Procrastination Equation*, researcher Piers Steel outlines many of these procrastination pitfalls. One thing he found repeatedly is that a person's energy level was directly related to his or her ability to focus and stay on task. But he also found that people who are constantly doing productive tasks or those they feel positive about wind up feeling that they have more energy. One positive of the one-day contract is that, by focusing on taking care of those things that need to be done and maximizing your efforts, you'll feel more satisfied and energized at the end of the day if you've met your own terms.

Another factor that causes people to procrastinate is fear. But I've found that many of us in professional settings are operating with far too much fear. A one-day contract requires you to be bold. In fact, once you begin to experiment with new strategies (like the one-day contract) you'll begin to be energized by the freedom that aggressive approach brings. You can't be afraid to experiment and try new things. As long as it isn't a money-risking venture, be bold in your experiments. Some things you thought would be great ideas won't work out as well as you'd hoped. Others you didn't think held much promise will be fantastic. But trying new approaches and examining their success or failure is what will enable you to learn and improve your performance.

The greatest example of drawing the value out of experimenting—good and bad—is the inventor Thomas Edison. The greatest inventor in American history likely failed more than any inventor in American history. Edison even lived in Louisville as a young man, where he failed as a telegraph operator and an Associated Press wire service worker. One night at work he was tinkering in the office and allowed battery acid to drop on the boss's desk. He was fired the next morning. Look, you may screw up at work, but you're never likely to do anything as bad as drip battery acid onto your boss. Lighten up and get aggressive.

We're going to learn much more from Edison over the next few pages. But first, I want to ask you if you're ready to sign a one-day contract? Not tomorrow or next week, but right now, before finishing this chapter. (Put finishing this chapter No. 1 on your list, however!)

You're not signing up forever, just for a day. Eliminate those energy-draining activities and begin to plot out your days with purpose. You'll still lapse into procrastination. But by starting each day with a new contract, you'll experience many more days that are productive and leave you feeling positive to get to the next one. It's a great tool, because there is no risk. You may have false starts. You may have one-day contracts that you tear up. Sign a new one tomorrow, and begin to hold yourself to the standards you know are necessary to reach your goals. You don't need to fear signing this contract. Do it today.

DON'T GIVE IN TO DISCOURAGEMENT

We already have talked about persevering through various kinds of challenges, but the one-day contract helps with discouragement in a different way—by placing our focus where it needs to be. Let me show you how things work if your focus strays from the one-day contract mind-set. This example shows how you can get caught up in long-term goals instead of day-to-day work, and how the resulting discouragement and failure can lead you to fold up and move on. I know the example well because it is from my own life.

I was president and coach of the Boston Celtics, a dream job if ever there was one. But in the midst of adversity and failure, I quit as coach. I walked away. (I offered to stay on in an executive role to help fix the problems with the team, but the franchise didn't want to keep me, and I didn't blame them. Things weren't going well.) My Celtics experience taught me many things. As I look back on it, I was living too much for the future. I was consumed with making changes and trying to do anything I could that would make me look good as an executive instead of coaching my players and just taking care of my work of the day. I had this huge contract and every day my overriding concern was living up to it. The contract hung over me, and under its weight I lost everything I needed to find success, particularly humility and patience.

That, it turned out, was a recipe for failure. I was focused on a long-term contract and all its consequences, pressures, and trappings and I lost sight of putting my head down and doing the work I needed to do.

Now understand, being on a one-day contract doesn't make every day a successful one. We cannot have unrealistic expectations that everything we do will be a smashing success. I experienced this several years back when we got knocked out by Morehead State in the NCAA Tournament's first round. We were up four with eight minutes to go when our best player, Preston Knowles, broke his foot. Elisha Justice, a walk-on, had to take his place. And although he did a serviceable job, he did not possess at that stage the talents of Preston. At the time, it was a disappointing loss and we took a lot of heat for it. But after a while, we had to stop making excuses for it, and accept that we lost to a great team. The one-day contract doesn't always wind up the way we hoped it would the night before. Still, we organize and plan going into each day as if our contract is expiring at the end of it. And that in itself helps you handle discouragement better.

Discouragement often comes from focusing on the wrong things. It also derives from a lack of patience, which is a virtue we are losing in our society. The one-day contract alleviates one of the biggest reasons people give in to discouragement—a misplaced focus on the future or the present circumstances instead of on the present task. I'm not asking you to sign up to achieve something a year or a decade from now. I'm asking you to sign up to make the most of tomorrow. That sounds far less formidable, right? Which of us can't plan and resolve to live and work one productive, efficient, successful day? It's within our power.

Things might not be going well, but if you can feel good about your preparation for the day, the effort you gave, and that you maximized everything you could that day, you are more likely to feel encouraged the next day and less likely to throw in the towel. The one-day contract takes care of the immediate goals and focus. But for concerns about what is down the road, you also have to have a building mentality.

Here's why a building mind-set is important: Many people, young people especially, look at the jobs they have and a rate of success that's slower than they want and they begin to give in to discouragement. But they're looking at it the wrong way. Sometimes people who quit on themselves too soon don't understand the concept of building something. They're on the lower rungs of the ladder looking up, frustrated that they can't reach things at the top. They fail to understand that it's not from the bottom that you reach those heights, but you have to pass through the lower rungs to get there. By sticking with it, you are building a résumé and laying a foundation. We had a national championship team in 2013. We were not a national championship team on the first day of practice in August. We didn't even look like one in January. There may be times you don't feel as if you are winning. The job may not compensate you well or challenge you or even be a job you're passionate about, but at some point you have to consider what would happen if your big chance presented itself and someone called to ask your boss's opinion of you that very day. If you've stuck with it, worked hard, given great effort, and earned good reviews, you're going to keep moving up. If the reviews are lukewarm, you're staying right where you are.

Sometimes people don't understand the value of the job they have, or of the time they spend in a single day of working. Phil Laemmle, a longtime political science professor at the University of Louisville, used to speak to every group of incoming freshmen. He gave a lively presentation in which he'd break open a can of biscuit dough and compare it to their impressionable minds. But one of his more pertinent illustrations was when he would show the freshmen a movie ticket. He'd hold it up in front of them and have them agree that if they had a ticket to the movies for a certain time and date, they wouldn't be likely to miss it. Then he told them that while they didn't have a physical ticket, each class session represented a similar opportunity. And he urged them to understand that if they wouldn't throw out a ticket to the movies, they shouldn't throw out that class opportunity.

My career in sports has borne this out. I have had teams go into the locker room twenty points down, only to come back and win the game. How were these teams able to accomplish this? First, they were prepared going into the game. They also were able to make the appropriate adjustments to give us a chance at a comeback. But more than anything, they had an attitude that they were not going to quit, that they were going to continue to play relentlessly. And they left the locker room thinking not about erasing a twenty-point deficit, but about executing the next play, scoring first, getting a stop on the first possession of the half, and making the adjustments the coaches had shown them in the locker room. Just because the game had been discouraging to that point, they were not discouraged, or at the very least did not give into the discouragement they were feeling.

How did those players in difficult circumstances keep from becoming discouraged? By focusing on the job they had to do, but also by realizing that success was within their reach.

Thomas Edison had more than ten thousand failures in attempts to invent various items. Surely, here was a man who had to have been discouraged at the end of many days. But here's what he said: "Nearly every man who develops an idea works at it up to the point where it looks impossible, and then gets discouraged. That's not the place to become discouraged."

Edison also said this: "Our greatest weakness lies in giving up. The most certain way to succeed is always to try one more time. . . . Many of life's failures are people who did not realize how close they were to success when they gave up." That is the subject we need to take up next.

DON'T QUIT

This is something I am seeing more and more in our society. People are folding in life like it's a game of Texas Hold'em. Dropout rates from high school and college continue to be a problem. Even in a time with high unemployment rates, government figures showed that there were months when more people quit their jobs than were being laid off or fired.

We have talked about difficult times. One of the most disturbing trends I see today is a tendency among people to give up on their goals and dreams entirely too soon, or to fold up when the first adversity presents itself. If people don't immediately see success, they think what they are doing is not for them. But look carefully at any successful athlete, businessperson, corporation, or sports team and you'll see that mentality is not a part of the culture.

A recent survey by ChurchLeaders.com diagnosed the leading reasons why clergy leave their vocation. They don't differ from reasons we've seen hindering focus and achievement in other areas: discouragement, failure, loneliness, moral failure, financial pressure, anger, burnout, health problems, marriage and family problems, and being too busy. All are obstacles, but none of those in and of themselves are reasons to quit. In fact, there are many examples of people enduring those and more yet still finding success right around the corner, because they simply stayed at it.

Succeeding in difficult times means perseverance, and that trait is not prevalent in these times. We are the now generation. We want success at our fingertips. Patience is ceasing to be a virtue. And let's face it, you can develop all of the wonderful traits you need to succeed—focus, humility, toughness, and passion—but if you quit when things become difficult or when you become discouraged, they all are worthless.

It has happened with me. I allowed things to get to the point in Boston where I was no longer effective, and where the town and franchise recognized that they could do better with a new start. I have experienced the cycle that leads to quitting. But I'm not alone.

David Petraeus was one of the most respected generals in the United States. From there he became head of the Central Intelligence Agency, and was recognized as one of the most important military leaders in our nation. When an extramarital affair became public in 2012, Petraeus quickly resigned and left the public arena. His reasoning, a military official told NBC, was that, "In his mind, in his views, with his code of ethics and morals, he did a very dishonorable thing." He believed that he brought dishonor to his position and undermined the trust the public had in him.

Although there is certainly truth to his statement, stepping down or leaving public service was not the solution. He was and remains too valuable an asset to quit on his country and himself. He made a mistake, and certainly no one knows that better than I do. You have to own up and face the consequences. Difficult times lie ahead in dealing with forgiveness from God and family. But he is a vital leader and should not compound his mistake by letting our nation down. Human frailties cannot lead us to quit, either on our jobs, our teams, or in this instance, our nation. From a military perspective, Petraeus's viewpoint may have been correct. But on a grander scale, look at what he would have been able to do with his ability as a leader. One would hope this talented general would return to a leadership role where he can contribute to our nation. There are times when your effectiveness is finished, and where moving forward would benefit no one. But that's not what we're talking about here. We're talking about adversity setting in and deciding to exit the stage when the benefit of sticking it out might be better for everyone involved. He surely knows his personal life better than anyone and he must chart his own path, but his departure leaves a great void, as does the loss of his experienced leadership.

Let's look at a leader who could have quit, but did

not. With the passage of time, Bill Clinton is coming to be viewed as one of our best modern-day presidents. Facing scandal of his own making and withering political pressure, he faced up to it and, in the end, not only had an extremely successful second term, but will go down in history as one of his era's most popular presidents. Even after leaving office, his influence and importance to his party have remained strong. In fact, you could argue that he remains the central figure of his party.

Let's look at the flip side: What might have happened had he stepped down instead of digging in and facing the painful public scrutiny? Imagine what might have happened if Bill Clinton would have walked away in disgrace. His post-presidential initiatives would not be what they are. His ability to help his party would've been destroyed. Even his wife may well have suffered in her ability to go on to become a U.S. senator and a highly successful secretary of state. The amount of charitable work Clinton has done with various global disasters might never have existed. His Clinton Global Initiative is active in 150 countries and expects to provide more than $73 billion in aid to people in need around the world. Let's understand, the most difficult thing about digging in is finding peace with God and your family and making sure they come first, before expecting any true resolution of the public situation at hand. But once that healing is under way, you can find a wealth of resolve to weather the present difficulties and turn them into future success.

I understand the nature of it. You are embarrassed. You want to run away, and you think it's easier to go away and hide because it may hurt less, but that is the direct opposite of the truth. Your problems don't go away like that. Once peace reigns again through hard effort with your family, with lessons learned you can come back better than ever. For those who feel compelled to quit because of regret, the greatest hurdle is earning forgiveness. Only time will bring that forgiveness and heal those wounds. And for those who feel compelled to quit because of adversity, how do you know that you aren't just a few short steps from turning the corner if only you will press on? There are many examples. Just look at the rewards, and what was accomplished by so many people by digging in and moving ahead and not giving in under pressure.

It hardly crossed my mind, when I was going through my turmoil with a pending extortion trial, to quit. I did say to my boss that I would do so if he wanted me to. But from the point he told me to never give that another thought, I dug in and fought and did what I thought was the right thing, and I wasn't quitting at all. Still, I have to admit, had I not gone through my Celtics experience, I might've handled things differently. I learned from my earlier failure that to succeed, you have to keep moving forward. And believe me, it's not easy. Learn from my experience. Part of the one-day contract is that you do not quit. You finish the day, and play to the final buzzer.

How many times have we seen in sports a situation that looks bleak, only to have success around the corner? What if Sugar Ray Leonard had said to Thomas Hearns after a few rounds, "It's not going well. Good fight, maybe we'll have another one," and packed it in? At Louisville, our own football team had a similar experience. It doesn't get much tougher than being down 14–3 in the middle of the third quarter in a hostile environment on the road with a Bowl Championship Series berth on the line. But it was worse than that for our team. Star quarterback Teddy Bridgewater was hobbled by a badly sprained ankle, and had a fractured wrist on his nonthrowing hand. It looked as if the Cardinals' hopes for a BCS appearance were gone. But within a span of thirteen seconds, that all changed. Bridgewater improvised a shovel pass to running back Jeremy Wright for a touchdown. Moments later, Rutgers fumbled the kickoff and a Louisville recovery led to another Bridgewater touchdown pass. Louisville fans went from despair to the Sugar Bowl in a matter of minutes.

At U of L, I've gone into the month of February twice in the past three seasons knowing that our team had to win eight out of our final twelve regular-season games to feel confident that we would reach the NCAA Tournament. It's a high-pressure situation. Usually, things had not gone the way we wanted up to that point. But never once did I think of not succeeding. I worked my one-day contract and practice by practice, game by game, we got to where we set out to go.

Discouragement cannot dictate your actions. People in these times need to redefine what gratification is for them.

Tom Coughlin is a good example. The critics were merciless. But he continued to work his plan for the New York Giants and won a Super Bowl that no one believed he could win.

The movie *Lincoln* was a box office hit. It's worth noting that this Kentucky native never won an election in the state of his birth. His political and personal difficulties are sometimes overstated, but it can be fairly said that he suffered both personal and professional setbacks on the way to becoming president of the United States, but did not quit in his quest for public service.

"I am a slow walker," Lincoln said. "But I never walk backwards."

Quitting is a deliberate return to square one. In a few cases, it is necessary. There are times when quitting is best for all involved. But for most in our society today, the quitting happens far too soon. Make a promise to yourself now—you're not going to quit. You might have bad days. You might get to the end of your one-day contract and feel like ripping it up. Don't quit. Sign another one and keep at it.

EXECUTING THE ONE-DAY CONTRACT

So let's say you've made this agreement with yourself. You've signed on the dotted line. What now? You'd better get busy. You have twenty-four hours to demonstrate your worth. The one-day contract forces you to prepare the night before, improving your performance with a plan of action for the following morning.

I am under contract at the University of Louisville until age seventy. But I've never paid less attention to a contract than the one I have now.

Starting three years ago, before retiring for bed, I would plan out the strategy for the next day's practices, and the motivation of all our players. I'm on my one-day contract. It not only stimulates my mind to be the best I can be for that day, but most important, it makes me realize how lucky I am to deal with a remarkable group of young men. I get excited for the next day at work before the day even begins. That makes me plan for every minute. It makes me prepare and it keeps my focus on those areas that I can control, areas that actually matter. I do that every day in this job—I have one day to make this team better, how do I attack it? Everything is organized, down to the texts I send players at night.

If the guys had a great practice, I'll text them saying so, telling them that it's what I expect of them every day, to get them thinking about the next one-day contract.

This is more than a to-do list. It is a mind-set that you train yourself to develop. Making lists and schedules is a must in leadership. I've done that my whole life. But a contract is something more. Think about what a contract entails. First, it is a commitment. You're signing on to do a job or to accomplish a goal. There are definite terms. It is an agreement to *do* something. There must be action. Your days of putting things off until tomorrow are over. Often, there are incentives, but at the very least, there is a concrete set of expectations. It's a binding document, and that's the essence of what I want you to feel about what you are doing when you wake up in the morning. You are committing yourself. When you sit down to negotiate a contract, your priorities must be clear in your mind. And when crafting your one-day contract, you will want to think about not only what tasks you want to complete or actions you want to take, but about what mind-set you want to instill, and what you are building toward in your day's work. And finally, there's an element of evaluation. Did you complete the tasks? On a to-do list, you might or might not get through your list. With a one-day contract, we're going to work on making your expectations manageable but achievable, and toward a larger end. Contracts can be altered, changed, or renegotiated, but they are always about getting the most out of your abilities. A contract is a daily challenge, and that contract that you are writing with yourself is about getting the most out of yourself every day, and getting the most out of your potential.

More than just mapping out your list of tasks for the next day, you should map out how you want to approach the day and its challenges, as well. In his blog on procrastination (at Procrastinus.com), Piers Steel cited a study by researchers for the Academy of Management Perspectives journal that surveyed two-hundred-plus working professionals. Workers who reported lower levels of fatigue and more energy used the following techniques at work: Learn something new, focus on what gives me joy in work, set a new goal, do something that will make a colleague happy, make time to show gratitude to someone I work with, seek feedback, reflect on how I make a difference at work, reflect on the meaning of my work.

As you build your one-day contract, these are things you might have in mind as guidelines. In addition to plotting out your day's strategy, remember to spread these things into your day. I had not seen this list until putting this book together, but I recognize many of these items, because they are things I find myself doing.

On the other side of the equation, the following actions are those that were found among workers who reported higher levels of fatigue: drinking caffeinated beverages, talking to someone about common interests, listening to music, surfing the Web, checking and sending personal e-mail or text messages, making plans for the evening or weekend, daydreaming, and shopping.

Here is how a typical plan in the one-day contract mind-set works for me, and I will use our first day of practice before the 2012–13 season as an example. Keep in mind, my goals are firmly in place—to focus squarely on the day at hand, to build a team toward national championship level, and to establish a positive environment around our program:

ONE-DAY CONTRACT: RICK PITINO

Terms: To lay the groundwork for a championship program, set a tone for improving from last season's Final Four run, and instill energy and a championship mind-set in players and coaches.

Points of emphasis: To be primarily positive in interactions with players and coaches; to listen; to improve on every single element of the day over the same day last season.

Schedule

6:30 a.m.—Meet with coaching staff. Be positive and energetic so that they will feed off that energy; challenge every coach to be better and have more of an impact on the program than they had last season.

7:15–7:45 a.m.—Meet with team trainers and strength and conditioning coaches. Listen to their input on where the team stands from a health and conditioning standpoint. Get them to buy into a one-day contract that challenges them to come up with innovative ways to improve our strength and conditioning. Leave them with this thought: If it's not broken, break it and make it better. We will have to do this if we want to reach championship level.

8:00–8:42 a.m.—First individual instruction session, with point guards. Emphasis will be on positive instruction and improving on workouts from a season ago. Go into each workout with the goal that it will be the best I have ever conducted.

9:00–9:42 a.m.—Individual instruction with shooting guards and wing players.

10:00–10:42 a.m.—Individual instruction with power forwards.

11:00–11:42 a.m.—Individual instruction with centers. The contract for each session of individual instruction is the same.

Noon–1 p.m.—Have my smoothie for lunch, and exercise for one hour. Last season, I exercised for forty-five minutes, this year it will be for one hour. Even though I'm one year older, I had already planned to make it one year better.

You can see as this unfolds, that the plan isn't just a list of tasks, but that there is meaning behind what I am doing, there is a motivational element, and that I am already writing into my contract from Day One the elements of improvement that will be needed for a championship season.

1:30–2:45 p.m.—Watch video. I committed to watching at least forty-five minutes of video per day, either of our workouts from the current season, game video, or tape of last season. I'll also do any additional organizing needed for the rest of the day.

3:00–3:15 p.m.—During this time each day, I will speak to our team for fifteen minutes on a different topic. It's just a little time to motivate our guys to be the best they can be between the lines, and to teach.

3:15–5:15 p.m.—Practice. These sessions are highly organized in themselves, with each drill and scrimmage scheduled down to the minute. They are crafted in consultation with our coaching staff to maximize all of the limited practice time we are permitted to have by NCAA rules. In addition, I have committed to make our practices more positive and energetic than they have been in the past. I approach these no differently from games. I need to be at my best, and diligent with each fundamental. This is part of my one-day contract. Attitude and approach to practice time might seem like something that could be taken for granted after as many years as I've been coaching, and it is. That is a danger. It's why I write into the one-day contract that I should be as passionate and serious about creating great practices as I ever have been.

5:30–6:30—Meet as a staff to review the practice. Again, this is a heavy listening session for me, to hear what the staff thought of practice, and then weigh in myself with what I thought.

Evening—I plan dinner with my wife, and after that to handle recruiting phone calls and text messages. Later, the plan for the next day is devised in the same way, renewing the one-day contract, evaluating how things went earlier in the day, thinking about ways tomorrow can be better, and then planning concrete actions to make it better.

Points to consider at the end of the day: Was I positive enough with staff and team? Did I improve upon the same days from last season? What does tomorrow's plan look like? If I were my boss, what would I say?

The contract, then, is more than a checklist of things to work through. It is a way to conduct yourself through the day. It sets your agenda and drives your actions. And it holds you to a high standard, which you renew daily.

My son Ryan is a good example of the right kind of approach. He's a twenty-two-year-old who is trying to make it in a Wall Street–type environment. We've talked about the nature of his business, and the knowledge that you're only as good as your last trade, and that you should keep yourself on a one-day contract.

So what does he do? He tries to be the earliest to work. He's prepared and he's early. All day, he asks questions, probing his more experienced coworkers as to how things could be done differently if they happen to go wrong or learning about what went right in the successful deals. I encourage him to find the people with experience and ask, "Can I buy you a drink after work? I'd like to get your insight on some things." Then pick that person's brain. I tell him to network. And even if people can't take you up on the invitation, many will appreciate the indication that their opinion is valued.

If they do accept the invitation, listen to what they have to say, don't try to give them the answers. So many young people today try to give you answers to the questions they have. Maybe that comes from insecurity, or the need to be seen as smart, but there's nothing better than listening. At the end of the day, I'm always asking Ryan if he sent a text thanking whomever he went to learn from that evening.

If you are a leader holding yourself to the one-day contract standard, you can share it with those people who work with or for you.

When I met with our players after their Final Four trip in 2012, I asked them what they thought of the Final Four and they all said, "It was a wonderful experience." And every one of them said, "We've got to win the championship next year." Now, everybody says that, if you poll any team. But I asked our guys, "How do we bring it to the next level?" And I let the goals come from them. As a leader, if you can let your people state the goals, then you're in a better position to do your job, which is coming up with the plan for how to go about it.

It's interesting. Sometimes as a leader you can state a goal for your team, organization, or sales force, and they'll think it's too tough to meet, or too unrealistic. But if you first ask those same people to come up with a realistic goal, they'll come up with the same thing you would have. And if they come up with a goal, you have a better chance of meeting it. Red Auerbach always told me he never would diagram plays in the huddle. He would say, "Russ [Bill Russell] or Cous [Bob Cousy], what do you think we should run?" He'd get suggestions, and then he'd choose the play. He would pick a different guy in every huddle, then go with his advice. He felt that once they made the suggestion, they were committed because they all were involved in the process. As a leader, the one-day contract can be of benefit not only to you personally but to those people under you. And it begins more effectively if those people are the ones stating the goals. Once they state them, you can follow along and bring them into your own success strategy by saying, "Here is our series of one-day contracts. Can we meet these day to day?"

I've always been very much into time management and looking for more efficient ways to do things. The one-day contract has been one of the best I've encountered in helping me to focus, and to make the most of the present. Whether you're working for yourself, or part of a team, if you hold yourself to a one-day contract there is no choice but to do it now where your goals and ideas are concerned. If you procrastinate, you fall behind in the race. The one-day contract mentality also will force you to be organized and to prioritize your efforts. That thought you put into your success, combined with your preparation, will breed confidence. It will help you see results, but also to keep any results in perspective. The one-day contract makes you more interested in your process and leaves you less likely to be thrown into discouragement or overconfidence, regardless of the final score.

Life isn't about having the perfect position or job that is made for you. More often, it's about succeeding at the job given to you, and it is about building your résumé and reputation in order to climb the next rung.

Do this today: Sign a one-day contract with yourself, then earn another day. Write your plan down. Account for the hours of your day on paper. Start with the basics, then refine it as you get used to the practice. At the end of the day, try to be honest with yourself. Ask yourself candidly, "Was this effort enough? Did I earn another day?" If you did, you're on your way. If you didn't quite earn it, tomorrow you will get closer, or get it right.

Work as if your future depends on it—because it does. See difficult circumstances less as dead ends than as turning points. And remember that victory is closer than you think. In all areas of your life, your health, your family, your job, the stakes are too important. You can't pack up and go home. Dig in and start your comeback.

6

The Power of the (Realistic) Positive Mind-set

As I watched Luke Hancock step forward to receive the Most Outstanding Player Award after scoring twenty-two points in the national championship game and I heard the crowd—the largest ever to watch an NCAA championship game—go absolutely crazy, I wanted to laugh. I remembered one of our home crowds giving an exaggerated Bronx cheer after one early-season game when Luke hit a three-pointer, as he'd struggled early while recovering from shoulder surgery. Yet here he was, in that moment, the most celebrated player in the country. He never would have been there without an unflinchingly positive mind-set. There are many examples of the power of positivity in life. Luke Hancock in the Final Four was a living, breathing example.

If you were not around, it is difficult to imagine how

difficult a trip that was for Luke. A lot of people in our fan base were down on him early in the season when he was still slowed by the effects of double shoulder surgery. It would've been easy for him to become discouraged, to lose faith in himself. He could've become frustrated or impatient because the healing process was long and painful. He would show up for practice every day unable to lift his shooting arm above his shoulder. Our trainer, Fred Hina, would slowly stretch him out and put him through a series of exercises, some of them painful, others basic, like throwing baseball passes with a basketball, to get his shoulder into playing shape. And this was a daily thing.

You'd think a kid dealing with discouraged fans and a difficult recovery would, at some point, give in to frustration. Luke never did. "He always showed up ready to work," Fred told me. "He's the toughest kid I've ever seen. Not many would play through the injury he had. But once he was convinced that his shoulder was getting better, even if it was slow, he came in and did the work with a positive attitude. As long as he did the work and was able to practice every day, he had confidence that his game would come back."

I don't know that you will ever witness a more confident player than the young man who made four consecutive three-pointers inside of two minutes with his team trailing by twelve in an NCAA championship game. Yet that's what Luke Hancock did. An effort like that is not only one for the record books—his five-for-five shooting from three-point range was a championship game record—it's one that deserves to be studied.

Coming out of a timeout, off an out-of-bounds play we had called in the huddle with 2:59 left in the first half, Luke inbounded to Gorgui Dieng, then took a handoff from the big man just to the right of the key and used him to get a sliver of daylight, knocking down a three to trim our deficit to nine. He hit another with 2:35 left, off virtually the same play, from the same spot, and pulled us within seven. The third was the result of pure point guard play. Peyton Siva ripped down a defensive rebound and dribbled the ball up the court. He saw Hancock trailing the play, moving toward his spot. Then you saw the genius of Siva, who took a couple of bounces in front of Hancock's spot, inside the three-point line, then turned and flipped the ball back to him, shielding off defenders. This one was three to four feet deeper than Hancock's first two. He swished it, and the deficit was down to four. His fourth in a row came off an out-of-bounds play following a one-handed offensive rebound by Stephan Van Treese. Hancock got the ball at the top left and tried a ball fake. Michigan's Caris LeVert didn't bite. Hancock started to dribble. He pounded the ball and moved toward the spot on the court, just to the right of the key, where he'd made three straight threes. Michigan's Jordan Morgan flashed out to hedge and bumped Hancock off his path at the top of the key, but then he turned to recover his position back in the lane. As he did, he screened LeVert off for just a brief moment—long enough to let Hancock pull the trigger from his favorite spot.

By that time, the entire Georgia Dome was on its feet. Those fans saw the four straight three-pointers. They didn't see the hours of work Luke had done rehabilitating his shoulder, the number of threes he'd taken from that spot, and they didn't see some other things, the confidence he had earned from his teammates because of his positive approach, and his positive influence on their lives. Notice how often teammates looked for him, or set screens to free him for a sliver of daylight to shoot. Everybody talks about Luke's four straight three-pointers. Fewer people remember Peyton Siva having three assists in ninety seconds. Luke's final three in that stretch was pure confidence, looking to trigger the offense, then seeing a defensive mistake and firing without hesitation.

Luke's positive mind-set came as a result of his toughness, his confidence, and his preparation. Those are not words you usually associate with the positive-thinking movement. Positive thinkers are usually identified as feel-good, I'm-okay-you're-okay pushovers. But in this chapter, we're going to talk about positive thinking in a whole new way. To start, I want to take you inside a couple of late-game huddles.

The first was at Boston University. It was late in a game that we had to win to make the NCAA Tournament. I got down on one knee and told the team, "Look, I'm going to diagram this play. The jump shot is going to be open, I guarantee it. They're going to expect Player A to shoot, but he's the decoy. We're going to get this wide-open shot. Make the shot, and we go to the tournament. We had this chance last year and we didn't make it. We can't let that happen again, where we don't get to the tournament. We're going to get a great shot, let's make it." Then I gave them the play and sent them out. But there was a problem. I wound up putting so much stress on that shot, and planting that negative memory of failure in their minds, that even though it was wide open, we didn't make the shot and we didn't make the tournament.

Fast-forward to another late-game huddle. This was in the midst of the so-called greatest game ever played, with my University of Kentucky team against Duke in the 1993 Elite Eight. The winner would go to the Final Four. I don't call too many timeouts in late-game situations to diagram plays, but we weren't prepared for that moment. So we had a huddle. I said, "Look, first thing we've got to do is get the ball in bounds, so form our box play. If Sean Woods is not open, we're going to do such-

and-such [we would have run another play]. But if Sean is open, we're going to get him the ball. Sean, I want you to get the ball and all you need to do is rip it down the middle. John Pelphrey is going to be open here, and we'll be having a guy coming baseline if we need to rebound. I'm not sure exactly what is going to be open, but you can make that play. You'll see the play to make." And before they left the huddle, I said one more thing. "Just do me one favor, guys. When we make the shot, don't celebrate. We don't know if they're going to inbound immediately or what they will run." Our guys left the huddle, and they made the shot. We didn't win the game because Christian Laettner made an even more incredible shot, but I had left our guys with a positive image going out onto the court, and they produced a positive result.

There's a reason there are probably more books on positive thinking than on any other subject in the Self-Help Section. Its power is demonstrated time and again in all our lives. You saw it in those two timeouts, totally opposite, two different ways of approaching a challenge—one by stress and intimidation, one by positive influence. That's why so many people have so many strategies for getting positive, staying positive, being positive. There are as many different strategies as there are people to employ them.

But in this chapter, I'm going to give you a different

key to positive thinking. In fact, let's look at this language. "Positive thinking" has been a catchphrase for decades, but recently it has come under a much needed critique. Barbara Ehrenreich's *Bright-Sided: How Positive Thinking Is Undermining America* showed some pitfalls of a blindly positive outlook. My coaching colleague Bob Knight addressed the subject more colorfully in his book *The Power of Negative Thinking.* Knight's point wasn't that everything needs to be negative, or that negative reinforcement is the only way. His point is that in order to achieve positive results, one must work for them, not hope for them. I certainly agree with that. And during the course of this chapter, you'll see that borne out. In fact, I don't even want to use the term "positive thinking." What I want from my players is a positive mind-set, and I define that as a positive approach based on confidence in one's ability developed through preparation.

You'll find no shortage of people telling you how important it is to keep a positive mind-set. I agree with all of them. And you don't need anyone to tell you the damage that negative people or forces in your life can cause. As I look back, whenever I've coached with fear and intimidation, something bad happened. In all the great comebacks my teams have made, including overcoming two twelve-point deficits in the Final Four on our way to the NCAA championship, our Marquette "Miracle on

Main" in 2012, our Kentucky "Mardi Gras Miracle" at LSU in 1994, or my 2005 team's twenty-point comeback to beat West Virginia in the Elite Eight, you name it, all have started with the same message, "We're going to win this; I see the other team tiring." The positive approach works, and it is proven time and again in every field. So it's a given that positive is better than negative.

But the road to positive thinking and living also is more difficult than many people make it out to be. In the 1980s, Al Franken made the character "Stuart Smalley" popular on *Saturday Night Live*. His character would sit in front of a mirror and repeat the phrase, "I'm good enough, I'm smart enough, and, doggone it, people like me." Too often, positive thinking in our society is reduced to the way you feel, or to putting on a positive face for the world to see. Too often, "positive thinking" is reduced to a mantra you can recite, or a playlist on your music player that you can use to turn your emotions in a positive direction. It's a poster you hang in your room or pithy sayings on a calendar. Now, I do believe that what you put into your mind is important. But it is not the ultimate key to developing a positive mind-set. Nor is any amount of hoping, wishing, or wanting a given goal or accomplishment. You can't will something to happen without working for it to happen. In his book, Bob Knight wrote, "Having the will to win is not enough. Everyone has that. What matters is having the will to prepare to win."

If you want to be a truly positive person, there is only one key, and that is preparation. That's the element that is missing from a great deal of the positive thinking discussion today, and it is absolutely the most important step not only toward establishing a positive mind-set, but maintaining it over time in all situations, including when adversity strikes. Today, we hear people talk about "having a bad hair day" or "getting up on the wrong side of the bed." A positive mind-set has nothing to do with either. The foundation for your positive outlook and approach to life does not happen by accident or luck. Your positive approach to life and work must happen on purpose, through planning and preparation. And once you have done the work you must do to be prepared, then all of these other strategies can have their full impact.

Someone once asked the legendary John Wooden, "How can I become an optimist?" Wooden answered, "Proper preparation and attention to details." There's a reason he won more championships than any coach. He knew that preparation was the key. In our program, we base everything on having a realistic positive mind-set and we try to avoid what I call the false positive. Our football coach at Louisville, Charlie Strong, calls it "fake juice." What we want in our program is the real thing.

We don't want people being unrealistic, but we want their optimism to have a strong foundation on preparation and work. Think back to your school days. If you had been in class all semester, taken good notes, done all the reading, and mastered the material as the professor presented it, then at test time you walked into the classroom with confidence. But if you skipped classes, did only sporadic reading, and finally pulled an all-nighter before the test, trying to cram a semester's worth of information into your head, no amount of positive thinking was going to help you on that test. You could have all the belief in the world, repeat all the feel-good words in front of the mirror, but those positive feelings, without the proper preparation, would not produce results.

We want a winning mind-set in our program. But we also want our people to understand the difference between being positive and putting on a smiling face. There's a fine line between being positive and being foolish. If you're down three with three seconds left, if you're prepared for that moment, then there's a very good chance that shot is going to go in. I've experienced it. If you're throwing a party or having a wedding or a business meeting or retreat, if you're prepared for any scenario, you generally have a great event. But any wedding planner will tell you, if you go into the big day saying, "It's going to be an awesome wedding," yet you haven't considered every scenario and prepared and planned for months, you're likely walking into a disaster.

Preparation, then, is the fuel that gives the positive mind-set its power. It's not the smile on your face or waking up in a good mood. I've gotten to know New England Patriots coach Bill Belichick. He's not the first person most people would point to if asked to give an example of a positive person in the NFL. But Bill is an extremely positive man, and a big part of that is because he's so well organized and prepared. Ask people to think of someone positive and they're most likely to come up with someone who is smiling and laughing, with almost a cheerleader mind-set. They think of the Dick Vitales of the world. They wouldn't think of a guy like Nick Saban. But again, he's a guy who is positive with his players, and who infuses his program with the confidence born of great preparation.

Take a look back at Luke Hancock. Everybody on the outside was down on him, but it was because they didn't see what was happening behind the scenes. Every day, he was putting in the work. And that gave him confidence that he was on the right track, no matter what the results were in a given game, or what people might have said about him. His positive mind-set wasn't driven by results or outside opinion, but by the actual work he was doing.

So how is all this accomplished? You must start

with the understanding that the realistic positive mind-set doesn't just happen naturally. It is something you must plan for, starting with how you go to bed the night before. You have to be thinking about the next day's positive mind-set before your head hits the pillow. The one-day contract is a great way to accomplish this. If you sign on for it, you will already have devised your plan for the next day and will have a strategy for moving in the right direction. The mind-set you go to bed with and the mind-set you wake up with are key factors. Your subconscious, while you are sleeping, will take whatever emotions you fell asleep with and run with them. During the season, this is especially important for me. I've found that a good book works better than anything. I switch off the news and any other negative influences that may creep in, and read a chapter or two of a worthwhile book on my way to going to sleep. Waking up "on the right side of the bed"? During the five to eight hours you sleep, your mind is going to take care of that. But it starts before you ever fall asleep, with your confidence that the next day you will get up and take care of things. We all know the anxiety and sleeplessness and dread that come with having a task for which we are unprepared looming. If you are unsure what is going to happen the next day, you will not be truly positive in approaching it.

Ken Lolla is our soccer coach at the University of

Louisville. He believes so strongly in going to sleep with the right mind-set that when he tells his children bedtime stories, he always plants lessons or messages into the stories. He has developed one such lesson into a successful children's book using that approach out of his desire to have his kids thinking the right things before they go to sleep, because it will have an effect on how they wake up, and shape the rest of the day.

Scotty Davenport was an assistant of mine at Louisville who went on to win an NCAA Division II national championship at Bellarmine University in Louisville. The night before every road game, at bedtime, Scotty sticks his head into the rooms of his players and tosses a candy bar onto the bed. Around the piece of candy is a note with a short message he wants the players to take into the game the next day. By tossing that candy in at bedtime, he has created a little ritual, and players expect the candy, and that note. But he also wisely plants the seeds of success for the next day with his players at that key moment before they go to bed. With text messaging, our coaching staff will often text players at night to set their mind-set for the next day, or text them in the morning with positive messages.

I have tried, over the years, to develop a positive routine for starting the day. I wake up around 6 or 6:15. I go downstairs and stretch a little bit. At my age it's a necessity. I do ten to twelve minutes on the elliptical machine. I'm going to do more exercise later—and I'm always building time for exercise into my daily plan—but I need to get my body going in the morning, and this is how I do it, just enough exercise to wake up thoroughly. Then I go upstairs and shower, and head to work. On the way to the office, I do not allow negative influences to creep in. I don't listen to talk radio. One wrong statement and you can be in a bad mood for hours. Why let that distract you from the job at hand? Often, I'll call up a good friend and talk for ten or fifteen minutes, anything to hear a positive voice and to get things off to an enjoyable start.

With our staff, we begin the day with a forty-five-minute meeting. Now I have to tell you, I've stormed into these meetings before and absolutely ripped everybody. Just ask some of my former assistants. These days, I'm making it my goal to begin those meetings on a positive note. I try to get guys to relax. I'll get coffee. I'll get breakfast. It makes a statement to your staff and that sets a tone for the day. Think about this. You plan everything else in your life—your retirement, your vacations, and your holidays. Does it not stand to reason that you have to plan your approach to the day as well? You will quickly learn that everybody around you will feed off your emotions.

And one challenge you will encounter is that it is difficult not to feed off the negative emotions of others.

We all know those people. We all encounter them along the line. For you, it may be a boss or coworker who simply drains the energy from the room, or whose constant carping makes it impossible to maintain a positive outlook. But even this you must plan for. You know going in that you cannot fall into that trap of despair. One useful tool is to try to understand how that negative person operates. It helps to try to learn what pressures they are under and to listen to them. You don't do this to let them influence you, but to try to "scout" what is motivating them or where their unhappiness comes from. In this way, you'll be less likely to be influenced by their negativity and more likely to view it as just another opponent to defeat during the course of the day. But more than this, it's important to keep your focus on your own goals and to understand that the reward isn't always praise from others, but what you are accomplishing with the work itself. If you're in the midst of a negative work environment, always keep this thought in mind—if someone from your dream job were to call your office that day and ask about you as an employee, what would your superiors and coworkers say? If they have no choice but to report that you are an extremely hard worker who approaches your job with enthusiasm and energy, you are halfway there.

With our team, when we are going through rough stretches, I repeatedly remind them on how they will be judged—and it will not be on their present struggles, but on how they handle those struggles and respond to them, and on how they perform at the end of the season. On the day I began this chapter, we were just days removed from having lost a basketball game when we were ranked No. 1 in the nation. Our senior point guard, Peyton Siva, one of the outstanding players I've coached in my career, committed a costly turnover near the end of that game that gave Syracuse a three-point lead in the final minute. I saw Peyton's head sagging and immediately called him over and grabbed him by the shoulder and said, "Forget about that. We're still in the game. We can make a three-pointer. We can win this." The turnover we would have to live with. The negative response we cannot live with. Sometimes it's not the actions of others that allow negativity to slip into our thinking. Sometimes it's our own mistakes. But even then we simply have to recognize what is happening, and realize that a negative response is only going to lead to more negative results. Our eyes have to be on the goal. It takes great effort to be positive.

Some people, of course, go the other direction. When they fail or are in the midst of negativity from others, they develop a false opinion of themselves. They take to social media for validation or start to take shortcuts. The work environment is toxic so you start to cut out early or neglect working the extra hours you should be working to get the job done right. In the end, this behavior is self-destructive. Tiger Woods, through his own behavior, derailed perhaps the greatest career in the history of the sport. But his work ethic and positive approach to a negative situation should allow him to make a comeback. Hillary Clinton lost a bitter primary election to Barack Obama. But she remained focused on making a positive contribution, accepted the position of secretary of state, and when she left her cabinet post held the highest approval rating of any national politician. Anytime I find myself drifting into a negative mind-set—and that happens to everyone—I realize that I'm on the road to failure. And more often than not, the way out of that mind-set is to get back to work, to better prepare myself for the situations that led to that negativity in the first place.

We talk about fundamentals a great deal in basketball. The fundamentals of preparation are the building blocks of a positive life. When I have players who haven't put in the work over the summer to strengthen their fundamentals, working on ball handling or post moves or their shot, they struggle to stay positive when the season begins. Chane Behanan, for example, is a physically very talented basketball player. When we started our shooting drills I noticed he would always get discouraged when the shot wouldn't go in. I repeatedly would say to him, "How can you get disappointed when you've never put in the time and preparation to be a good shooter?" It always befuddles me when I see a player get disappointed by a shot not going in or when he doesn't execute a move correctly when he never put the time in to master his shot or perfect his moves.

One trap of traditional "positive thinking" is that it sets up false expectations of happiness. I appreciated the work of Barbara Ehrenreich, who became weary of being told to "think positively" about her breast cancer diagnosis and treatment. She wrote her book in response to it. She wasn't railing against attacking your problems or working for positive outcomes, but she was challenging the positive thinking industry, and rejected the notion that her cancer was a "gift" and that she'd be healed if only she stayed positive enough. Sickness and tragedy are not gifts. But my viewpoint of the realistic positive mind-set is that you have two choices, to attack them positively and in the process hope to encounter or become something worthwhile, or retreat into despair and negativity, into a state that benefits no one. I've done both in my life. Sometimes you need to go through the stages of both. But the positive mind-set, based on life, and our experience, and our preparation and toughness, bids us to move forward.

There's one more aspect of the positive mind-set we need to consider, and that is being a positive influence on others. Everyone wants to attach themselves to positive people, and as soon as adversity hits the fan, people want to run the other way. The easiest thing in the world to do is to denigrate others. That takes no talent. There are people in this world who have immense talent, but because they are so critical and negative, people run the other way. You can't be overly critical in your professional dealings. You can't be self-serving. Having a positive mind-set is not only about yourself, but also about others around you.

In my profession, negative recruiting is rampant. It's not enough for some coaches to make their recruiting pitches; some coaches feel the need to put down every other school while they're doing it. I'll never forget my greatest lesson in this, which came in 1976. As a matter of fact, that experience is the source of a rule I still have today when I sit down with a recruit and his family. It all started in Nashua, New Hampshire, where I traveled on a recruiting visit for Syracuse. I remember it so well because Jim Boeheim and I have laughed about it so many times over the years. I was recruiting Rich Shrigley, a power forward at six foot seven who had the ability, on a lower scale, to play a lot like Tyler Hansbrough of the Pacers plays today. He was just the type of young man you'd want on your team. Jim hadn't seen him that much or communicated with him. I said, "Jim, when we go in the home, I've got a great relationship with the mom and the young man, let me do most of the talking with this one." I felt good about our chances. Remember, we were in New Hampshire, not on Tobacco Road, and I knew very well that it was down to North Carolina State and us.

During the course of the conversation with Richard I said, "One thing I've noticed about Jim as a head coach is that he has an eight-man rotation, and those guys get most of the minutes. There are some other programs that fill all fifteen scholarships with players who could play at any program, then wind up playing only ten or twelve of them. Take N.C. State. Coach [Norm] Sloan is a great coach, and certainly they have a legendary program. But they have fifteen players who can play, and how do you fit into that program with fifteen guys?" I told him it was just a matter of numbers, and we didn't have such big numbers and he'd have a better chance to play at Syracuse.

All of a sudden, Rich's mother, who had been listening very attentively, said, "You know, I told Norman about that, and Norman has too big a roster and we've talked about that with Norman." At some point I stopped her, because she was using the coach's first name, and I said, "You're talking as if you really know Coach Sloan." She smiled and looked me square in the eye and said, "Yes, the reason I talk to him so personally is he's my brother." As Jim fell off the couch laughing hysterically, I wanted to crawl underneath it. I realized at that point, although I hadn't been negative about Coach Sloan or his program, that would be the last time I would mention another school or coach to a recruit. From that point on, all recruiting would be about our program and what we had to offer. And it's been easy to remember that lesson, because Jim Boeheim never lets me forget, whenever we get together. Negativity can accomplish nothing good. Others can point out playing time or contrast you with a competitor. You would be wise to stay away from it.

Does this mean that as coaches, we never use negative reinforcement with players? Well, all you have to do is watch any coach on the sidelines to realize the answer to that. I will get into a player who is doing wrong. I will get into a player after a mistake, or one who is not responding in the right way on the court. I'm not advocating a life in which everyone is praised all the time, regardless of performance. And I'm not advocating that you live that way. Sometimes your honest opinion is asked of you. My only advice is that in a professional setting, deliver such thoughts constructively. Be a positive force where you are, and let your actions or, if necessary, your criticisms, come out of a team mind-set.

An extreme in behavior made headlines in the coaching profession during the 2013 season. At Rutgers, a young basketball coach was caught on video shouting antihomosexual insults at players, shoving them and throwing basketballs at them. This, of course, is unacceptable behavior. It is over the line, and the coach was removed from his position and is seeking treatment for anger issues. But it is the exception, not the rule. While we get on players in a heated way, especially in the thick of competition, we're always mindful that the goal is to prod them to do their best. In the national championship game, I was all over Peyton Siva, quite possibly the nicest young man I've ever coached. I was prodding him without mercy in the title game, because we needed so much from him. I'd say, "Are you tired? You must be out of shape. You're really looking gassed." The truth, and he knew it, and he knew what I was doing, was that he was turning in a performance of athletic endurance that I could never even have dreamed of as an athlete. After the game, and after many such exchanges this season with Peyton and Russ Smith, I made it a point to say to the press that I marveled at what those guys could do physically and the shape they are in.

I'm a coach. It's not always going to be sunshine. Sometimes, we're going to deal with negative behavior or negative performance with negative feedback of our own. Sometimes, it's appropriate to be negative. But the goal, always, is a positive outcome. It is never to hurt someone or to beat them down. The vast majority of coaches understand this. When they get after players, it is to push them to their potential. I've gone to bed some nights and actually felt guilty over how hard I got on a kid like Peyton Siva, because he's not only such a nice person, but he always shows up the next day smiling and back in his positive mind-set. I have great respect for Peyton. I'd feel bad not for things that I said, but that I pushed him so hard. Yet his ability to handle those things and his daily positive mind-set showed what happens when positivity meets toughness. That's when you get a champion.

So the true keys to the positive mind-set, in reality, have nothing to do with your mood. They have nothing to do with how you feel. A positive mind-set comes out of a deliberate effort. It comes through the preparation to breed confidence in what you're doing. It comes through planning, whether it's plotting out your day the night before, or paying attention to how you end the day; it requires your thought and attention. And finally it's about the projection you make to others, not out of a false sense of superiority or any kind of arrogance, but out of a desire to advance your own strengths and talents, and the unique things that you have to offer the world. There's nothing easier to find in this day and age than people who are hypercritical, snarky, or just plain mean. Meticulous planning, understanding how to attack your competition, and reaching back and never giving into mental or physical fatigue are the key ingredients that will steer you toward a positive mind-set. With all of that, if failure sets in at any point, you do not deviate from understanding the ultimate goal, and that is reaching the championship level of whatever endeavor you are attacking.

7

Heeding the Signs

After late road games, Father Ed Bradley would stay over at my home and leave early the next morning for his home in Owensboro, Kentucky. The late arrival back always had the same ending for us. We would sit downstairs and reminisce over old times at the University of Kentucky and at the University of Louisville. Father Bradley sat on the bench for eight years at Kentucky and now has done so for twelve seasons at Louisville. As we talked about the great games played, eventually the topic came up of why players would not see the signs for success and failure. Father would say he just didn't understand why Player X would take that path and not be able to see things that were right in front of him. He listened intently to the locker room meetings where we told the team if they travel this road, it would produce great hardships. If they take the other road, it would lead to success. The "why" question would always pop up. Why would you choose the road to failure?

The longer I coach, the more I'm convinced that the people who have the most sustained success are those who are best able to heed the warning signs and changes in their chosen professions, and who figure out how to stay ahead of the curves that life can throw. Early in my tenure at Kentucky, as well as Louisville, we recruited players like Tracy McGrady, Jermaine O'Neal, Sebastian Telfair, James Lang, Donta Smith, and Amir Johnson. They would make commitments or even sign with our program, then go to the NBA without ever playing for us. It was a double loss for us, because not only would we not get the talented player, we'd have no one to take the roster hole they left. Over time, I began to heed the sign that though recruiting the most talented players with the highest pro potential was appealing and something I'd done throughout my career, the trend of many elite players—or those who thought they were elite—to go pro before playing college basketball was going to hurt our program. At that point, I decided that the best way to move forward was to make sure I used a method that had always proved successful—to get a substantial amount of our talent into its junior and senior classes. Even after the NBA passed its age limit, forcing many of the elite players into at least one year of college basketball, we have built our program on the multiyear player who is committed to college basketball first. We certainly have and will take young men whose goal is to spend only one or two years in college, but we do not build the program around them. In looking back, our most successful teams at Louisville have been keyed by players who spent significant time in our program, players like Francisco Garcia, Terrence Williams, Earl Clark, David Padgett, Peyton Siva, Kyle Kuric, and Gorgui Dieng, among many others. Along the way, by developing individuals, we've had the good fortune to see players like Preston Knowles and Russ Smith rise from obscurity to a very high level.

But without heeding the signs, seeing the trend in what recruits were doing, and reassessing our own strengths and what we as a coaching staff and program wanted to be about and what we do best, none of those things would've happened. If we had continued to chase players who didn't fit our philosophy, we would've missed out on some great people and accomplishments.

Part of being focused is being able to perceive the signs around you. For most of us, "Stop" and "Go" are simple enough. We encounter them on the road. There's no choice involved. The more difficult signs are those that we see and interpret for ourselves. "Caution" signs require us to make a judgment. We see a speed limit, and determine how closely we will stick to it. In life, we all can read the signs when major crises force us to stop or leave a situation. We're not as good at seeing the other signs, whether from the input of others or looking realistically at our own performance and results.

For some reason today, we have become less able to read the warning signs around us. We've become accustomed to having the GPS tell us how to proceed on the road, but when it comes to heeding the lessons of others, or the advice of those more experienced, we are less willing to adjust our course.

Nobody exemplifies heeding the signs and making the proper adjustments better than Michael Jordan. MJ came into the league with an electrifying first step and mesmerized everyone with his aerial artistry. But "Air" Jordan was not at first known as a shooter with great range. He was a gifted scorer from the midrange who could get to the rim on anyone. But as he got older, he saw the signs of age and its effects on his abilities—a little less bounce in his step, and little less quickness—and developed new ways to be successful. If his signature image in the first half of his career was the spread-legged silhouette in flight we all know so well, the trademark of the second half of his career was a lethal fadeaway jumper. He developed that jumper out of necessity, heeding the signs of what time was doing to his game, and finding other ways to succeed. Instead of overwhelming defenders with speed and athleticism, he read defenders like a book, shot over them when they backed off, went by larger players when they tried to press up, or backed down smaller players when they played up on him defensively. By becoming a serious student of the game Jordan remained effective late into his unmatched career. Along the way, he also became one of the great defensive players in NBA history.

There is value in being able to see the signs. Anyone who has been successful at anything over a long period of time, whether they realize it or not, has read a series of signs and successfully navigated through them. But for everyone who has successfully managed to heed them, there are tales, sometimes tragic, of those who did not.

Everyone in Brigantine, New Jersey, knew about Lester Kaplan. He was intelligent and a daredevil, seventy-two years old, a gambler with a long gray ponytail who liked to swim as far out into the ocean as he could. In November of 2012, when the warnings of Hurricane Sandy came from sources all around his town and state, Kaplan ignored them. Time and again he refused pleas to leave his home on flood-prone Lafayette Boulevard in Brigantine.

Four days after the superstorm hit, firefighters found him lying on his living room floor. They'd been unable to get to him sooner. A day earlier, President Barack Obama and Governor Chris Christie visited the hard-hit town to survey the damage while Kaplan's family members still were barred from getting back into the devastated community. Kaplan, all the while, was suffering from hypothermia and near death on that floor in his home, without heat or electricity.

By the time they found him, it was too late. He died in an ambulance on the way to an Atlantic City hospital. Fire crews had been on his street just hours before the storm hit. They told Kaplan to leave with them. "We were right there if he wanted to leave," a fire captain said.

I'm reminded of a tale I've heard ministers tell. A man is stranded on a desert island and prays to God to be rescued. Soon after, a fishing boat floats up to shore and the fishermen ask the man if he wants to leave with them. "No," he says. "God will deliver me." A little while later, a helicopter sets down in a clearing on the island and those inside offer to take him to safety. "No," he says. "I've asked God to save me, and he will." Finally a seaplane lands off the shore and the pilot calls to him to come out. "No," the man says. "God says he will save me." Of course, the man dies on the island, and when he meets his maker, he asks, "God, I asked for deliverance from that island and truly had faith that you would help me. Where were you?" To which God replies, "I sent a boat, a helicopter, and a plane for you, what more do you want?"

It's true that quite often the signs are there for us to see. We must not only recognize what they are, but we must be able to see past our own goals and desires to recognize them.

There are several key components for heeding the signs in our lives and careers. The greatest asset is experience. I've coached basketball more than thirty years. It's rare in my field that I encounter anything that I haven't seen before. I can see the signs of a player who is distracted, or who is veering off course. The problem is that the player doesn't see the signs. It's no different from someone just starting out in business. Everything is new. How can that person be expected to recognize signs of good or bad?

I want to talk to you a little more about Gorgui Dieng. He's a remarkable young man from Senegal. He arrived in this country in 2008 not speaking a word of English. He admits to going into his room while attending a West Virginia prep school and crying because he was in such a foreign place. But in addition to being six foot eleven and a talented athlete, Gorgui is also an exceptionally intelligent young man who comes from a culture of humility and mutual respect.

I had talented players on the same team who have been immersed in American basketball culture their whole lives, who have had the same NBA dreams as Gorgui and enough talent to make those dreams a reality. But Gorgui is different in this respect—he was able to read the signs. He was able to recognize his strengths and weaknesses, listen to the input from coaches (who gave him input from NBA scouts and executives), and use all of that to map out a plan not only for his own improvement but also for reaching his goal of playing professional basketball.

Other players, however, who received the same input interpreted the signs differently. NBA scouts liked one of our young players very much, but gave me the feedback that they didn't like his body language. When I told the player, he didn't accept the criticism. He immediately started making excuses. He responded with, "Well they haven't seen my whole game," and other rationalizations, instead of seeing the truth in their advice, that over the course of an eighty-game schedule, you don't want to deal with someone with bad body language, because that belies a bad attitude. In discussing his game with him, I asked him, outside of his scoring around the basket, what else in his game had developed? Jump shot? No. Rebounding? No. Defense? No. Communication on the court? No. But he seemed to want to focus only on that part of his game that he thought was good, and considered anyone bringing up his weaknesses to be overlooking his obvious strengths. Now, as he gets older, he will come to realize that his response to those signs is wrong. Yet so many young people do this today, and even some older people, though perhaps for different reasons.

I started wondering why that was. Why should Gorgui, a foreigner with almost no knowledge of the inner workings of professional basketball, be better able to read the signs than a player who grew up around the game? I asked Gorgui what it was about his upbringing that enabled him to do that.

"How I was raised, we got told, when someone older than you talked to you, you don't have a reason to speak to him back, whether you think he's right or wrong, because he's older than you and has more experience," Gorgui told me. "I just learned from there. People are different here. They get criticized and just get upset. But I think if you listen, you have a chance to understand the game, if you listen to the right people. Like I listen to you. You know the game and know what is best for me to learn. If I don't trust you, and trust what some guy in the street tells me, then I'm stupid. But a lot of people I meet now, to be honest, they don't listen. They go through the motions. All the time they are watching YouTube and don't take time to learn. You always say we can't focus in for a minute.

"Where I am from, we were educated differently. We had to pay attention. When I took my friends to Senegal, they could not believe it. I sit on the floor. I read a book. You don't have to ask who is older in the room. The older person sits in the chair, the younger on the floor. Even if a person is only a year older than me. So you have to have respect for people, and you have to listen to people. I see a lot of people have freedom in school here. In school there, when the teacher talks, you write it down, you don't talk. They will whip you in school with a belt until age sixteen or seventeen. You learn to listen. And listening is the key. People here have so many options. When I have free time, I go play soccer or basketball. Then I go back to my house and study. I don't have any Xbox or video games, or TV. All I have is my books. We went to school Monday through Saturday, eight to twelve and three to six. And it gets dark. We don't have lights everywhere. So you stay in, and you study. We don't have parties on Thursday nights. You don't go to the restaurant to eat. Everybody cooks, and you eat with your family. A few people have phones or iPads, but not many. But the way we learn, we learn from our elders. My thinking is if I want to be a basketball player, I have to learn from Coach P."

Gorgui is able to read and interpret the signs because he respects those who have experience, and because he understands the power and value of listening. His experience can teach all of us the textbook approach for seeing the signs—a willingness to listen, openness to criticism and instruction, and finally, the ability to study our field and learn its particular warning signs and markers of successful people who have gone before us. Gorgui went from a player who weighed only 185 pounds and had no developed shooting or passing skills to a first-round pick in the NBA Draft, taken twenty-first overall by the Utah Jazz before being traded to the Minnesota Timberwolves.

For any young person starting out in a career, I would suggest finding five successful people in their chosen field to study closely and, if possible, to talk to for advice. Some of these might be people at the very top of the profession, whose work habits, mistakes, and successes can be studied from books or media accounts. But it's always good to identify these types of people in your immediate situation, people who are seasoned pros at the type of work you want to be doing, who can literally point out the danger signs and pitfalls of the road you are about to try to travel.

As coaches, we all learn from our mentors, and from those people in the game who are the most successful, who everyone tries to emulate in some way or other. With our players at Louisville, we try at times to do the same thing, to show them players who mirror their abilities and physical talents who have made it to the highest level. My players have probably grown tired of me showing them video of Kenneth Faried of the Denver Nuggets. His work ethic during games, his ability to go after rebounds outside his area, his technique, and his tenacity in never taking plays off, is something I've urged every player on our team to watch, respect, and emulate. Gorgui has watched it and embraced the lesson. Others are slower to accept it. Maybe they think they are more talented, or that their way is better. And maybe they are so distracted by other issues in their lives, with school, relationships, and families that they just don't take it to heart. They listen to what I'm saying about Faried, but they don't hear it. They interpret what the coaches are saying as "they don't like my game," instead of realizing it for what it is, information that they need to accept for their own good.

So just seeing the signs isn't enough. You have to know how to read them, and how to interpret them. We have players who will watch Faried and see the lesson, but will not interpret it correctly. They interpret it as a knock on their games, instead of as a tool for improvement. So it's not enough just to study, to find your five examples in your profession and scout them as if you were preparing for a championship game, but you must then do the right thing with the information.

Over time, it's also useful to come up with what you find to be the five signs of successful people in your field, the five warning signs, the five go signs—when to proceed—and the five stop signs.

In few places do you see these principles on display more clearly than on Wall Street. Consider the notion of a "bubble investment," that is, an investment that looks good initially, but eventually crashes. The bubble bursts. A famous recent example is the dot-com bubble. From 1997 to 2000, tech stocks and Internet-based companies saw their stock prices soar. It got so big that companies could just add the prefix "E-" to their names and see their stock value increase. But in 2000, the bubble burst. Some companies failed. Some declined drastically. Some fell hard, only to recover over time. So what were the characteristics of that movement? And what were the warning signs that so many failed to see? First, there was the dramatic rise in price. A skyrocketing price doesn't have to mean an investment is headed for a fall, but those who have observed Wall Street over the decades know that stocks behave a certain way over history, and when they don't, something is wrong. Second, there was a great deal of hype surrounding the investments. You couldn't open a financial magazine or read the business section of a paper without hearing about the dot-com boom. Those were signs, frankly, that were easy to miss. Who doesn't want to catch a stock on the way up? Who doesn't want to be involved in the latest hot investment?

But the third indicator is the greatest warning sign. Independent financial writer Miranda Marquit put it best: "Everybody seemed to be ignoring the fundamentals." If you're focused on the fundamentals of your job, your head will not be turned by the latest thing, which might or might not be the most beneficial thing. In the case of dot-coms, everybody got so focused on the skyrocketing price that they didn't look at the boring old fundamentals—price/earnings ratios, profits, company management, and political currents," Marquit writes. "It's not a lot of fun to look at cash flow and debt, but it's important." And the final indicator that people often miss is the mentality that "this time things will be different." Like the college basketball player who ignores what scouts are saying because he believes somehow he's "different," this mentality will keep you from reading the warning signs in your life. There were people who sounded the warning signs of a housing bubble long before the market crashed in 2008, but many believed housing was "different" from other investments, and could never be brought down.

From the financial world, then, we learn the importance of studying past behavior, of not taking popular trends at face value but investigating them more deeply, of never losing sight of our fundamentals, and of not deluding ourselves because of what we want to believe, but instead looking and listening for realistic signs of how to proceed.

It's a difficult concept to explore in specific terms, because not everyone is looking for the same signs. But I can tell you this—if you're distracted, that's warning sign No. 1. There are signs all around us today. In addition to literal signs, and the flood of advertising and marketing we deal with on a daily basis, there are messages bombarding us from family and friends, from the media, and from the workplace. That makes it all the more important that you consider this concept, and begin to craft your own criteria for seeing the signs. There's no substitute for experience, but by reading, studying, listening, and paying attention, you can begin to create your own map, and your own ability to recognize the warning signs that come your way, and your ability to heed them.

As coaches, we are constantly called upon to heed the signs our players and teams are sending us. As a coach, you must have your hand on the pulse of everything that happens, and you have to be willing to alter what you are doing. That came into play during our national championship season. After our five-overtime loss at Notre Dame, I needed to refocus our players in a positive direction. Our goals were no different after that loss than they had been before, but we needed to restate the goals in a way that would get our guys looking at them once again in a positive way.

Sometimes, to avoid discouragement, you have to take a new look at your goals and sometimes even refine them. With any goal, along the way you're going to have pitfalls. With our case in the 2012–13 season, the pitfalls were four losses. Now certain losses shouldn't shake a team's mentality in moving forward toward its goals. But unfortunately, because of the surrounding environment that we have in sports, you may have to redirect your goals. We lost four games. We let one slip away in the final moments to Syracuse. At Villanova we were up by eight and went on a barrage of missed free throws, and that was our downfall. Then we lost to Georgetown in a hard-fought game. They won because their slow style of play was better than we could handle. But it was the flip of a coin. Then we lost to Notre Dame because of a mishap on our part, and Notre Dame made some phenomenal shots to end regulation. In all four situations they were winnable games. As a coaching staff, we didn't panic, because we've been through it hundreds of times. But the people we were leading could have their confidence shaken by the outside environment that suddenly was questioning them. Our guys were getting questions from the media like, "Are you as a team going in the wrong direction?" They were looking for causes for why we were losing.

So I went to the team and redirected our goals a little bit. We redefined our smaller goals, with the big one still very much in sight. We talked about winning our final seven regular season games, getting a double-bye in the Big East Tournament, winning that tournament, playing close to home in the NCAA Tourney, and not cutting down any nets until we won it all. Your goal is to create optimism. When you redirect or revise your goals, that's what you're looking to do. The media was creating pessimism around our program when it lost four games; that planted seeds of doubt in our players. Our job as coaches was to counter that with an optimistic message. When I listed all those goals for our players, as I kept going on and the goals kept getting tougher, a fascinating thing happened: All the heads started nodding in agreement, because they loved the optimistic approach. They all bought in, because everyone loves optimism. They could see themselves achieving it.

The ability to see the signs is something we talk about with players. Especially within the course of a game, we are always telling guys to be alert, to watch for signs of fatigue in our opponents, or shortcuts they might be taking that we can exploit. In our NCAA Tournament huddles, I repeatedly said, "If you see something, if you see you have a weak defender on you or you see something that's there, let me know." In a crucial part of the NCAA championship game, Peyton Siva said to Luke Hancock, "Luke, the lob is open. They're not helping. The center isn't helping and I'm open." We scored twice on lobs to Peyton because of that. And after noticing and acting on that weakness, we were in a timeout, and we were able to do another thing. I said, "Luke, we're going to run that again and the guy on you is going to jump over to help on it. You can take the big guy on, or you can come off to the wing and hit a three." And he did make a big three.

Certainly, as a coach, you have to watch for the signs your own team is sending you. During the past season, if I noticed a guy was tired, I'd call him up to the office and ask him about it. Then I'd tell him that I wasn't going to sit him down for practice, because I didn't want to make all the other guys upset. But what I would do was put them through stretching with every-one, and then just sub them out of drills, so that they did no more than 10 percent of the drills on that given day. Over the course of the season I did that with al-most everyone at one time or another, so they all knew what was going on. But it allowed me to rest guys with-out worrying about a negative effect on team chemistry.

Developing the ability to read what you are seeing and alter your plan accordingly is essential for any suc-cessful venture. And heeding the signs is a practice that will serve you in all of life.

In 1980, a man named Harry Randall Truman became a celebrity in Washington state. There were volcano warnings all over the place. But Harry wasn't moving. He told anybody who would ask him, in his own eighty-three-year-old, salty way, that he was stay-ing, right there with his Mount St. Helens Lodge and his sixteen cats. On the TV news, over the radio, and in special notices distributed to residents by authorities, residents were warned to get away from that volatile area. Harry Truman listened to them. But he did not heed them. His defiance made him a celebrity. He even was flown out by helicopter on May 14, 1980, to talk to a school in Salem, Oregon, to answer questions and sign autographs. Then they flew him right back onto that doomed mountain. Four days later, with Truman ignoring the signs and sitting in his home, the side of Mount St. Helens blew off and Truman and his home were no more. They made T-shirts and bumper stickers commemorating Truman's stubbornness. You can probably find them there today. But that's not something to be remembered for. Make no mistake, life and our professional landscapes provide us with many important signs every day. We should not wait until things blow up around us to heed them.

Celebration after beating Michigan for the national
championship. *(University of Louisville Athletic
Department)*

Coach Pitino and
wife, Joanne,
watch *One
Shining Moment*
after the national
championship game.
*(University of
Louisville Athletic
Department)*

Rick Pitino at the team hotel after the national
championship victory.

(University of Louisville Athletic Department)

Rick Pitino with the colorful Russ Smith.

(University of Louisville Athletic Department)

The Pitino and Minardi families after the University of
Louisville's victory over Duke in the NCAA Midwest
Regional final.

(University of Louisville Athletic Department)

With the championship in hand, Rick Pitino and Peyton Siva manage a smile.

(University of Louisville Athletic Department)

Celebrating with Peyton Siva after the title win.

(University of Louisville Athletic Department)

The coaching tree, which includes every assistant who
has ever coached for Rick Pitino.

(University of Louisville Athletic Department)

8

Meaningful Distraction

For years I've been stealing a line of Woody Allen's and giving it my own twist. Woody is a huge New York Knicks fan and attends a ton of games. One time, somebody asked him what being a Knicks fan meant to him, and he said it was a "meaningless distraction." Over the years, as I've coached teams and interacted with fans and drawn from my own experience, I've come to the conclusion that for many of us, sports are not a meaningless distraction, but a meaningful one. As a coach, I've seen countless examples of sports enriching the lives of people, whether it was people, even children, with severe illnesses, or just people involved in difficult day-to-day situations who drew enjoyment, escape, and even inspiration from following a favorite team or sport.

This is an important principle in maintaining focus

and keeping your edge over a sustained period. You have to find ways to get away, to relieve the stress of your constant striving. If you're working with full commitment toward excellence in your job and life, then you not only deserve to get away from it all at times, you need it. Meaningful distractions are not a luxury in life, they are a necessity.

We've talked in this book about several kinds of destructive distractions—things that take you away from your task at hand for no good purpose. We discussed it at length in the chapter on technology. That's not the kind of distraction we're talking about here.

A meaningful distraction is one that brings you enjoyment and leaves you with more energy when you take part in it. It is completely separate from your job. It could be anything—a hobby, a pastime, the arts, reading, writing, music, fitness, for some it is philanthropy or public service—whatever removes you, even for just a few moments, from your present trials, gives you enjoyment, then allows you to come back to the job refreshed and recharged. Meaningful distractions help you stay on top of your game.

During our national championship run, everyone talked about how great our team chemistry was. I felt that a trip we took to play some preseason games in the Bahamas in August of 2012 was the start of not only re-creating our brand, but of all that great chemistry.

Our players got away and had a chance to interact with all our coaches and their families in a nonbasketball setting. They interacted with each other in water sports, fishing, snorkeling, and other things, and from the standpoint of us as coaches getting to know the players and them getting to know each other in a different light, that trip played an important role. It starts with something like that, just a one-week trip, and they came back with a totally different feeling about their teammates and coaches.

The benefit of hobbies or other kinds of meaningful distractions is well documented. People with well-established hobbies are generally healthier and less likely to develop depression. Dr. Michael Brickey, in his book *Defy Aging,* says hobbies (meaningful distractions) are a key component in staying mentally young. He says ideal hobbies are those that develop into a certain expertise over time, activities that draw on passions already within us, and those that connect us with other people.

I'll give you an example from my life. It's no secret that I dabble in the horse industry. For me, it's the perfect meaningful distraction. Horses don't race very often. If you're lucky, your horse will race once a month—if he is healthy—and they don't run twelve months a year. Obviously, during the season, I don't have time to go to California or Florida to see a horse of mine run. But I can turn on my computer, watch a two-minute race, and be removed for a short while. In that time, I'm caught up in the horse, how he's doing, whether he's a long shot or favorite, and when it's over I celebrate the win or shake my head at the loss, but I'm not affected one way or the other by the outcome because it's a pastime, not a life's work.

During the national championship run, a horse I own a stake in, Goldencents, won the Santa Anita Derby to reach the Kentucky Derby, where he became one of the favorites. When I got back to Louisville, reporters were asking all kinds of questions about next season, and I finally had to put on the brakes. I told them we had ten days of Kentucky Derby activities, and then the race itself, and I was going to really enjoy that. Over the summer, I'll start rolling again and figuring out offenses and defenses and the wheels will start turning. But I needed to enjoy the championship and that Derby experience.

And the Derby was a blast. The anticipation of the race, the experience of sharing it with friends and family, and all the festivities surrounding it were not only very exciting, but as much fun as I've had at any Derby. It led up to the race on a rainy day with a muddy track. Our trainers thought the conditions would certainly help our horse, being a front-runner. But he struggled mightily, and had mud kicked in his face, which he did not enjoy. I don't know how that is possible! I guess if we were having mud kicked in our faces, we'd understand. After the race, people kept apologizing and felt bad for our dismal results. I just laughed, had another mint julep, and said, "This is not my vocation. This is my vacation, and my hobby." And we just laughed and continued to have a good time. This is what a meaningful distraction is all about, getting away from the rigors and pressures of your everyday vocation, and it was a great getaway for ten days.

Through horse racing, I've been able to meet so many tremendous people, to not only make friends, but to share the experience of going to the races with friends and family. It has connected me with many people, and gives me something to look forward to whether things are going well with basketball or not. People kept asking me what it would have meant to win the Derby. It would've been great. But the reward of an experience like that is the entire process. Having friends into town and renewing relationships; throwing the Derby party; telling stories and making new memories. That's the reward of the Derby. It's different from basketball, which is my job and life's passion.

Now, you may not have the Kentucky Derby. But there is something you have, an interest, a love, something that draws your attention or intellect like no other thing. It may have nothing to do with your field of work or study. You might be a corporate executive who loves going to plays or restoring old cars. Whatever that distraction is, it becomes valuable when you give it meaning.

It is important for all of us, I think, to be a fan of something. It makes us a participant in the game of life. Idleness leads us astray, especially in this day of proliferating distractions. It puts us into a state of mind that's not healthy. Having that distraction leads us back to the life we all want; that great pressure that leads us to prominence.

I want you to think about something. After national tragedies, whether it has been 9/11 or the Boston Marathon bombing, what were some of the most moving public events after those awful occurrences? I think you'll find that many were at sporting events. The moments of silence. Crowds singing "God Bless America" after the 9/11 attacks. The Fenway Park rendition of the national anthem after the marathon bombing, with all 32,000 people singing "The Star-Spangled Banner," was very moving. These show the positive sides of sports, their power to give people a positive outlet for expression, to rally around something, to feel like part of something big and meaningful. After these tragic events, our patriotism and love of country come out more than ever. You can't tell me, if you've ever been amid such a crowd, that sports are meaningless.

In fact, not even Woody Allen would make that argument anymore. In 2012 the subject came up again in an interview with *The Wall Street Journal.* In this interview, Allen revised his statement on his view of sports as distraction. He told the *Journal,* "The Knicks are one kind of distraction. For the two hours you're at the Garden you're only focused on that. I follow them. I go. I have been a season-ticket holder for many years. They have not been very exciting. It was a nice little flurry for a while but then [Jeremy Lin] got hurt, so we'll see what happens next year. I am a big sports fan, baseball and basketball, everything. People will say to me, 'Does it really matter if the Knicks beat the Celtics?' And I think to myself, 'Well, it's just as important as human existence.'"

He went on to explain himself, and he did so by saying he has an idea for a movie about two directors—one who makes comedies or musicals, and another who is focused on very serious, high-minded, confrontational dramatic subjects that take on society's biggest issues. There might have been a time when he thought, like most people, that the director who was putting out serious content was doing the more important work. But now he's not so sure.

"You are living this terrible life," he told the paper. "It's hot. It's sunny. The summertime is awful. Life is miserable. You duck into the movie house. It's dark. It's cold. It's pleasurable. You watch Fred Astaire dance for an hour and a half. And it's great. You can go out and face life, based on the refreshment factor. If you see the confrontational film, you have a different experience and it seems more substantive but I am not sure it does as much for you as the refreshment. A couple of laughs, a couple of dance numbers, and you forget all that garbage for an hour and a half."

In the end, Allen said, who is to say which is more meaningful? That's my feeling, too.

I'm proud of my players for winning a national championship. I'm more proud of the fact that if you look at them individually, you can learn something positive from the way every one of them developed and persevered over the course of a season or a career. If you followed our team this season, you encountered Peyton Siva as a person and saw the kind of quality he exhibits, and you learned about his life from numerous media accounts. You watched him play as a point guard, always striving to make his teammates better, but you also read about his life in the many media accounts of his backstory, learning that Peyton is the kind of person who tries to lift everyone up, that his assists are not limited to the basketball court.

I can go right down the line on that basketball team. Russ Smith, Gorgui Dieng, Luke Hancock, Kevin Ware, many of their stories are at various places in this book because all of them have a compelling story to tell and, whether they won games or lost them, you had to come away impressed with who they are and the effort they were putting forth. As a fan, I would hope that following this team gave you much more than just a good or a bad feeling after a win or a loss.

Frankly, if it's just about the wins and losses, if that's all that matters as you're sitting in the stands, I think you're missing something. There is a type of sports fan for whom players are simply robots in uniforms. They aren't real people. It's all about being on the right end of the score so that you can feel better about yourself and maybe rub it in with the people at work. And all that is part of sports, I know. But you shouldn't feel any less self-worth if your team loses a game. I remember a funny situation with a caller to my *Big Blue Line* radio show while coach at Kentucky. The fan told me he was breaking down video and saw certain things in our offense with underneath out-of-bounds plays and had a few ideas. I interrupted him and asked if he was married. He was. I said, "Okay tonight, instead of breaking down film, open up a bottle of wine, snuggle up to your wife in front of the fireplace, and just see where that takes you." He called me the next week and told me he opened the wine, put the chairman of the board, Frank Sinatra, on, and snuggled up to his wife, and after a short while he couldn't resist. He got back to his game tapes and had some ideas about our future games. This gentleman is what we call a fanatic. They take it to a new level. It was extremely funny, but unfortunately, or fortunately, we have many of these who follow Louisville basketball, too.

There's a certain segment of fans today who show up at the game to take out their aggression and hostility. It's not healthy. If you feel the need to berate a college player, or even coaches, there's something wrong that needs to be addressed. If you feel the need to get on referees—well, that's all right. I'm kidding. But I can't blame people. I've gotten on a referee or two myself. Here's the takeaway—the goal of being a sports fan should be meaningful distraction. Sports should enrich your life. I've had restaurant owners and business owners tell me that if Louisville or Kentucky loses a game, the receipts are going to be lower that night. There's anecdotal evidence all over the state. If the home team loses, you might see fewer people at church, fewer people at the malls, fewer people out eating, managers might know that productivity won't be as high the next day.

People tell me that in this town there are radio shows totally devoted to denigrating our university. When I was at Kentucky there was a radio personality named Jock Sutherland, who Bill Keightley, our longtime Kentucky equipment manager, appropriately nicknamed "Mr. Wildcat," used to fume over. And I would ask Bill, "Why would you listen to something that makes you irate? That lacks common sense." He couldn't explain why, but it would boil him until his face turned red. He'd say, "You just don't understand this Jock Sutherland." And I'd tell him not only did I not understand him, but I didn't want to listen to him. I don't want to get in a bad mood. I don't want to get upset at a man I don't even know. Why would Bill listen to a man who would denigrate Kentucky basketball around the clock? But there are fans here in Louisville who will do the same thing with a host that denigrates Louisville basketball. And all I can say is, "Why do you listen?" And fans will answer me, "I'd like to punch that guy right in the nose." I can only ask them, why would you feel that about somebody you don't even know? And more than that, why do you even listen if he makes you feel that way? It doesn't make sense. That's not what being a fan is all about, working yourself up until you want to hit someone. It's about raising your self-esteem, coming away happy, and feeling like you're part of a worthwhile effort.

I've never seen our town, and our fans, so together as after our national championship. I've never seen anything like it. Yes, it's been twenty-seven years in coming, but that's not the entire story. I think they really enjoyed seeing our group of guys playing this Louisville First brand of basketball and displaying all of the great attributes that we saw from them. I think they came away with a special feeling for this group, and rightfully so. I think our team played the game for the right reasons. And as our fans gathered in celebration, they realized what this team was all about and they thoroughly enjoyed it. That is truly a meaningful distraction. From the Big East Tournament title to the national championship, our fans get to celebrate these accomplishments for 365 days. Why fans would go the other way and look for things to be upset about is beyond me. If you want sports to be a meaningful distraction, look for all the positives in sports.

There are so many examples, however, of fans going the other way. I've seen just about everything in sports. We've all seen stories of fans behaving badly, and not just at pro sports events, but also at college and high school. There are some who will spew the most venomous language and behavior you can imagine. It's almost, for some, an acceptable forum in which to espouse hatred. But for me, sports need to be about the relationships you build over years and years of being a fan. They need to be about feeling like you're part of the process, so that when your team is down, you want to do something to lift them up, rather than do something to put the players down even more. They need to be about learning from victory and defeat, and whatever happens, going back to your work and family and life feeling energized, not demoralized.

As the price of tickets increases, people more and more feel that they have the right to abuse the players on the court or the coaches. As a coach, I accept that. I'm paid to handle all of that and still do my job. I would just hope that more fans would view their allegiances as a meaningful distraction in their life, and to treat them that way, as something that makes their lives richer.

There's one more kind of meaningful distraction I want to discuss. In the chapter on focus, I mentioned some studies out of Harvard that showed even a small break every two or three hours can increase a worker's productivity. Well, that also holds true on a larger scale. To stay at the top of your game, it's best to figure out a way to take extended time away from work to refresh and recharge the batteries.

Your life has to consist of a diverse portfolio. Any financial planner will tell you that you can't have all your money in one place. The same thing is true of the human body and how it works. There are so many people throughout history who have burned themselves out. The coaching profession is full of them. Your body is just like an automobile. The parts get worn down when they're driven too hard. You certainly want to be passionate. You certainly want to uncover everything available to have a successful team or business, but you must take time away, and it must happen with people who are going to lift up your spirits and emotions. Surrounding yourself with positive energy and people is essential when you do take time away. The opposite— negative energy, cynical people—will just drag you down and that time away will be nothing but misery for you.

When the season comes to an end, I will take all my children and wife to something special. This year we're going out to California, to Los Angeles, then Santa Barbara, and we'll take eight to ten days as a family. I save all year for this and we go overboard. I do that with family members. I take two vacations, the first with family members, who have helped and sacrificed for me throughout the year, even the grown children. Last year I took my sons on a golfing trip and all the girls wanted to go to Paris, and they went by themselves. And later in the summer, I make sure I take two days here and there with guys I work with, our trainer, my assistant, our sports information director, and I'll take them on a weekend trip. Then I'll take a few other guys to Del Mar or Saratoga and give them four or five days as my treat. These are people who put in the time right alongside you, but don't get the financial gains.

Some people can be generous with money, but generosity is more than just the trickle-down effect of making sure people are taken care of financially. Generosity also is the act of making sure people have a great time. You have to be generous with your time when you are able. It's important for me to get people away from the workplace, to talk to them about what they might like to see different with their jobs and what would help them perform better daily. In doing that, I am able to learn what their needs are, but also to see that they have a good time, enhancing their meaningful distraction, so that they can come back to work energized. We talk about family. If we talk about work, it's usually just to talk about something we can laugh about, but I definitely get the input to make our workplace better the following year. All of these times away give you something to look back on fondly when work gets stressful, and they also can give you something to look forward to if you're committed to saving for them. It's one thing to hand somebody a check. But being generous with your time is just as important.

It's also important to take time away for your own health. A lot of people think the most important thing is rest and recuperation. The way we go at it, twelve- to fourteen-hour days, with great intensity, that time away is essential.

I play golf, but I don't look forward to playing golf. For me, the best thing is every summer I take two weeks and go to Del Mar or Saratoga, and I will just spend most of my time people watching. I enjoy the characters at a racetrack. I love to watch people yelling at television screens. I love hearing the excuses after a horse doesn't come in. I just sit there for nine races, and just go around and laugh with the bartenders or the waiters and waitresses who've heard it all. When the race is over I listen to all the explanations. A good friend of mine, Joe Iracane, after every single race has this elaborate story about how he could have made a killing. I tell him I could've made a killing if I'd had tomorrow's newspaper today. But he's been doing this for fifteen years, and we all laugh about it. For me, it all goes back to laughter, more even than sleep and rest. When I take time to get away, I want to create laughter in my life. I'll invite someone like my great friend Ralph Willard, who was an assistant coach of mine with the Knicks and Kentucky, as well as Louisville. We have laughed together for forty-three years. Whether it's on a daily basis or a weekend away, creating laughter can make all the difference.

I even turn fund-raising trips into occasions of laughter. I do about ten trips a year that are auctioned off for us to fund-raise for our basketball program. On 50 percent of those trips I take along people with whom I wind up building future friendships in addition to adding supporters for Louisville basketball. It's not a chore for me. Meeting different people and sharing experiences with them is also a good learning tool for me. I never get tired of these experiences. When you do get away, you can't let the people you're with make it feel like it's a burden to you. Enjoy what you are doing. Go overboard and you build support for your effort.

And what's true for me in terms of getting away also is true for our players. They need time off. I am deeply concerned because the AAU circuit has guys playing year-round without a letup. I suspect so many knee injuries today are from chronic overuse. You can't play three games in one day, with two hours' rest. The AAU circuit is putting wear and tear on their bodies, so that by the time a lot of these players get to the NBA, if they make it, they have older bodies. It is essential for players to get off their legs. And what's true for them physically also is true mentally. There's a breakdown that occurs when it's game after game after game. Our guys take three weeks completely off, and when they come back we encourage them to do thirty-five to forty minutes in the weight room and thirty-five to forty minutes of skill work, but I don't want them pounding their legs playing a lot of games, because the season is going to do that for them. We build in time off for our players during the season and during the offseason. When we travel during the season, we try to take time to talk to them about everything, to have an environment of laughter, when it's the right time to laugh, and to be serious when it's the right time to be serious. Young people today have no shortage of distractions, but we do try to give them time away from the demands of basketball, too.

Now, I understand. Most people are not going to own horses. Maybe your resources are such that you can't take people on trips for days at a time. The principles, however, are no less true. You can develop your own meaningful distractions. You can be generous with your time with the people around you. It might not be a weekend away. Maybe it's one night and a round of golf. Whatever the case, finding time for your mind and body to be away from the demands of work, and trying to help those around you to do the same, is a major tool in maintaining the kind of focus you need to succeed.

There is no question, taking time away and cultivating meaningful distractions make you better at your job. They keep the stress of work from wearing out your body and mind. Every time the president goes on vacation, people criticize him. But with the demands of that job, if he did not get away, you'd have a worn-out man leading the country, and we don't want that from our president. We should be encouraging the leader of our country to get away with his family from time to time. If you don't take time away, you will succumb to burnout. You will see your passion wane. You'll mentally drain yourself and it won't be fun anymore.

If you are a tired, worn-out person, you look at adversity differently. You become demoralized more easily. Not only is this kind of distraction important for your focus, it's important for your ability to get out of difficult times when they do strike. A tired, fatigued person makes mistakes. So look at your life. Examine your passions and opportunities for time away. They are not just luxuries you hope to make "extras" in your life if you find time. They actually are necessities that you must carve out time and money for, as much as possible. Once you return from these meaningful distractions, you're excited and eager to get back to work. They can be the times that stir your passion and give you the spark to achieve all those goals you want to accomplish.

9

Prospering from Pressure

The most asked question throughout the entire NCAA Tournament for my basketball players, as well as for me, was, "Can you feel the pressure?" We were the overall No. 1 seed. We were the favorite to win the championship, and with each round, as the other top seeds fell by the wayside, the pressure and expectations only increased. Did we feel the pressure? You better believe it. But we didn't just feel the pressure—we loved it. As a coach, the pressure on our players was in many ways my best friend in the task of helping to prepare them for those tournament games, each with stakes higher than the one before. Pressure is not stress. Pressure, in fact, is little more than a tool we must use to reach our potential. So many times, getting the most out of our abilities is itself a by-product of the pressure we face to perform. I had no hesitation about putting pressure on our players. In fact, I gave them the stated goal, after we had lost for the fourth time in seven games in the five-overtime heartbreaker at Notre Dame, of going undefeated the rest of the way, all the way to the national championship. Did that put too much pressure on them? Yes, if you believe pressure brings about stress. We do not. We believe pressure is your ally. It forces you to concentrate and execute. It makes you mindful of the kind of effort you must put forth to reach your goals.

It was put so succinctly in an interview renowned journalist Lesley Visser did with Billie Jean King, who won twenty Wimbledon titles. Leslie asked if that pressure had ever gotten to her. King's answer was awesome: "Pressure is a privilege, and one that should never be taken lightly."

Pressure, in fact, can reveal greatness in you that you did not know you had. It is an extreme case, but I want to take some time to consider again the story of Kevin Ware. With 6:33 to play in the first half of our Midwest Regional Final against Duke, Ware faced one of the great crises of his life. He came down from a closeout and landed awkwardly on his right leg. I stood in front of him and watched him leave his feet. He came down and I thought my eyes were playing tricks on me. It looked like something popped out of his leg. I bent down and extended my hand to help him up. My eyes then became as big as church bells. Kevin noticed what I was looking at and his eyes focused on what we both saw. He bellowed out, "Oh my God." His bone was sticking about six inches out of his shin. Our players came over and as they saw, started crying and getting sick to their stomachs. Our equipment manager, Vinny Tatum, and trainer Fred Hina got to Kevin and both moved to put a towel over the exposed bone. While a lot of our guys were upset out on the court, Luke Hancock came to Kevin and took his hand and told him he was going to say a prayer for him. Shortly after was when Kevin's exclamations went from shouts of shock to shouts of strength. He told me, "I'll be fine, Coach. Just win the game." Then he started saying it over and over. He was afraid his teammates weren't hearing him. He asked if I'd get them over there. "I'm fine. Just win the game," he repeated to them. Again and again he said it, stronger each time.

It was remarkable and became an international story. Of everything that transpired in college basketball last season, Kevin's injury and response were the biggest story. And I say it that way for a reason. Lots of players sustain injuries, some of them even on television. But Kevin's response, and the response of our players, showed such character and compassion that they captured the emotion and attention of the nation.

Pressure, in this circumstance, revealed something

in all of us, but most of all in Kevin. Here's a young man who early in the season was suspended. He was sullen, mistrustful of adults. And suddenly he experiences this one event, and the change is breathtaking. I'm not talking about phone calls and notes from celebrities. I'm talking about Kevin's entire demeanor. He has become a gregarious person. The pressure of that powerful moment made him a man who has outgoing skills, who has a personality to communicate with a lot of people, from being on Letterman and delivering his lines flawlessly to going out and speaking—effectively—to groups of people. We didn't know that was within him. He didn't know he had all these talents. They were hidden. And they might not have come out, or would have taken longer to come out, if not for these events, and his courage in dealing with them. In that five-minute period, he witnessed a teammate praying over him, he saw the emotion of his teammates and coaches, and he suddenly felt that incredible love that a family has when someone is suffering, and it changed his whole personality. He went from a player who rarely looked coaches in the eye to one who was writing on Instagram about his love for his coach and his view of him as a father figure.

Kevin is proof to many people that you never know what you have within you until you put it to the test. And sometimes pressure is exactly what is required to put you to the test. I know many people will hear and accept this message, because many already have.

People all over the nation have written to Kevin. Old and young, wealthy and poor. He has received letters from people in prison and from those who have injuries similar to his. What is it that prompted such an outpouring? It wasn't just the severity of the injury. It was the inspired nature of the response. I often wonder what would've happened had Luke Hancock not come alongside Kevin and prayed for him in that moment. Kevin himself gives Luke credit for settling him down, and in that moment, Kevin said, he realized he had a choice to make. He could think of himself and allow himself to be crushed by his misfortune, or he could think of his teammates and all they had worked for, and try to say something that would enable them to press toward their goal. Luke's prayer didn't heal Kevin in that moment, but you can't deny that there was power in it, even if only in the act of a teammate kneeling down beside him to offer support. The calm it instilled in Kevin truly was life changing.

If you ever need proof of pressure revealing character, just look at Kevin Ware and what happened in the aftermath of his injury. Not only was there the *Late Show,* but he received a phone call from First Lady Michelle Obama. Many professional athletes in all sports reached out to him. He was invited as the guest of CNN to the annual White House Correspondents' Association Dinner in Washington, D.C., where he got to hear the president deliver his annual roast of the media.

But it isn't until you see some of the notes sent to him by people that you understand the power of his actions, and I believe, the power of this very subject; that is, the power of pressure or even misfortune to make us more than we were before.

Jonathan Espinoza Valencia, an eighth grader in New Castle, Colorado, wrote to Kevin, "You are like the older brother I never had and all of your teammates are like my brothers. . . . You are my hero and your injury inspires me just like it inspired your team to win it all."

Jessica McGivern of West Deptford, New Jersey, wrote to him: "I'm writing to you to show how much of an inspiration you are to me. I recently just recovered from an injury, a ten percent tear to my Achilles' tendon and a broken growth plate. . . . I also hurt myself during a playoff game, by an illegal pick. Just like your team, my team won it all, leaving a big smile on my face. I live by your quote, 'A minor setback to a major comeback.' It is getting me through all the excruciating hours of rehab. . . . I just wanted to say you are an inspiration to me."

Mail bin after mail bin, stories came pouring into the basketball offices of people who saw Kevin's injury and his response to it and were moved. The next time someone tells me, "Nobody sends cards and letters any-more," I'll tell them they need to look at Kevin Ware's mail. There was a card from a woman in Lexington who had a horse fall on her leg, fracturing it in a dozen places. She sent encouragement with the news that she had recovered. He heard from Portland, Oregon, and Portland, Maine. And he heard from college athletics teams all over, from the Alaska-Anchorage athletic department to the Maryland lacrosse team.

So many children were moved to write to him. One, from Goshen, Kentucky, couldn't yet write, so she drew him a picture and wrote her ABCs on a piece of paper. A woman in Ann Arbor, Michigan, was getting ready to watch the Wolverines play Syracuse in the Final Four when CBS ran a feature about Kevin. Her little daughter watching the telecast became interested and started asking questions about it. At around five o'clock, she started writing Kevin a note. The mother wrote one, too, just to let Kevin know how the story had made an impression on her little girl.

Justin Erpenbach of Elk Mound, Wisconsin, wrote to Kevin, "The way you fight every obstacle in your way has inspired me to try in sports 100 percent harder. The way you handled yourself in this incident absolutely amazes me and tells the world how good of a person you are and how good your character is. Also I was amazed at all the media attention you got, and how you handled it so well and were thanking everyone for caring about you."

Brian Jaquette, a Duke fan with two degrees from the school, wrote, "I don't think most people would be able to think, much less talk, while they were in as much pain as you must have been. But to tell your team to go out and win and not worry about you is just amazing. Even though you weren't on the court, I'm sure your words did as much as any player to lead your team to victory. I want you to know that I will be rooting for Louisville at the Final Four and during your recovery."

A young man named Mitchell Marcus sent Kevin a special message. Mitchell, a special needs student, was a student manager for four years at Coronado High School in El Paso, Texas, and before his last game as a senior, his coach surprised him by telling him to suit up. Late in the game, not only did his team do everything possible to allow him to score a basket, the opposing team finally saw what was happening and backed away to allow the special moment to happen. The video became a YouTube sensation and was seen all over the nation and world as an example of sportsmanship. Mitchell, in turn, wrote to Kevin, and told him he was praying for him.

I recount all of these letters, and all of these people, because I want to emphasize the importance of this lesson. Sometimes we see pressure as a nuisance. For

Kevin, though he didn't know it at the time, it was an opportunity. It was a vehicle for revealing something within him that may not have been revealed in any other way.

Kevin got a handwritten note from Mike Krzyzewski, and a letter from Bill Clinton, who, in handwriting in the lower margin, wrote, "You inspired the country."

Marquette coach Buzz Williams sent Kevin a small card of the type he gives his own players. On it were the words: "It's not hard to live through a day if you know how to live through a moment."

That is true. So many of our players are proof that pressure can produce sterling results. When pressure strikes, don't miss your moment. Pressure is not your opponent; it is your catalyst and friend.

In this book, I've told you about Luke Hancock responding to injury and adversity. But there are others. So many of our players were forged by the pressure of different difficulties or responsibilities in their youth. Peyton Siva's father was absent for much of his childhood, and his siblings were in trouble. Somehow, Peyton lived in that world but was not of it. He went to Bible studies and dragged his friends along. When his friends were having hard times at home or school, Peyton would take them home with him. The stories of Peyton, at thirteen, driving the family's car to find his father on the streets of Seattle and rescue him from a wayward life have been told often. For much of his childhood, Peyton felt the pressure of being the one in the family who held it together, and through that became, with Billy Donovan, one of the finest individuals I've ever coached.

You can go right down the line with our guys. Gorgui Dieng came to this country from Africa feeling the pressure to succeed for his father, his role model, who means the world to him. Chane Behanan has told the media that he feels like he might be the last hope for his family's well-being, after growing up in poverty with one brother in jail. After his family's home burned down, a grandmother decided Chane needed to leave that environment to move to Bowling Green with some family. When he did that, he also changed his commitment from Cincinnati to Louisville. Chane not only credits that with changing his life, but with saving it.

Wayne Blackshear had to battle back from injury. We had to hold him out for about a week of practice during his freshman season because the NCAA was still looking into his grades. When we went to the Final Four in Atlanta, he had the highest cumulative grade point average of any nonfreshman in the field, and won an NCAA award because of it.

During the Big East Tournament, Russ Smith was devastated when his high school coach, Jack Curran, of Archbishop Molloy in New York, passed away suddenly.

He sobbed on our team bus, and struggled with the passing of a great man who understood him, saw the potential in him, and always believed in him. Right then, I told Russ he should dedicate the rest of his tournament to his old coach, and that's what Russ did. He responded by scoring twenty-eight points in twenty-nine minutes that very night to lead us past Villanova in the Big East Tournament quarterfinals.

It was the beginning of our postseason run, a run that would not end until we cut down the nets in Atlanta. But we did not look like a championship team in the first half of our title game against Syracuse in Madison Square Garden. We fell behind by sixteen points, as many as we had trailed by all season, and were down thirteen at the half. I told our guys we were losing focus on our game. I asked, How did we prepare to attack their zone? They gave me the correct response. I came back with the statistic that we were shooting 29 percent and there was no attacking the middle with the pass or dribble penetration after ball movement. It was a road game, as the Garden is Syracuse's second home court. So it was going to be difficult. I even left the players to themselves briefly, after asking them if this was how they planned to represent us, with the instruction to figure it out before they went back out onto the court. We left the locker room with a strong conviction that we would come back and take that last Big East trophy back to The 'Ville. We attacked the middle with a double high post. It gave us high-percentage shots that led to our full-court press bothering Syracuse into turnovers. After trailing by sixteen in the first half, we won the game by seventeen. We left NYC with a special feeling but no nets were cut down. And we had a special visitor in our locker room for a second straight year. President Bill Clinton thrilled our guys by taking pictures and congratulating them. We were headed full steam toward the NCAA Tournament, with all that pressure following us like a shadow.

In 2012, we traveled to Portland, Oregon, with about a hundred of our fans. This time it would be different. We headed eighty miles east of Louisville, to the home of the Kentucky Wildcats. Most places roll out the red carpet when they host the NCAA Tournament, complete with motorcycle troopers getting you to your destination and preventing any traffic problems. Not Lexington. We joked that our escorts not only would not turn on their police lights but they would slow down. The only time the lights would be on is when they escorted us out of town. That statement couldn't be closer to the truth. We could sense the disdain for us with every forced hello. But we found it funny and laughed about it for a few days. Our hotel was full of professional people not getting caught up in the rivalry. It was great to see Rupp Arena full of Cardinal fans. I personally never have paid much attention to the rivalry on either side of the ledger. When coaching Kentucky, I just felt Louisville was another big game on our schedule. The same holds true as head coach at Louisville. UK is another tough game. Now, our fans do not subscribe to my beliefs. The rivalry was built with racial overtones. Louisville was the minority university, UK the white-dominated student body. But that was years ago. The rivalry today is not built on race—just pure hatred. That silliness is only for the deep-rooted majority. That small minority that I'm part of believes it is good for the state to have both teams exude excellence.

Our games in Lexington proved to me that our guys were dialed in. We approached North Carolina A&T with great respect and our defensive pressure was outstanding. Russ Smith grabbed an NCAA Tournament–record eight steals. Our second game, Colorado State, worried me to death. They were the best rebounding team in the NCAA Tournament field and had one of the best assist-to-turnover ratios. But our guys were completely attuned to the scouting report. We set a record for one of my teams, topping the seventy-deflection mark, in beating a very good team by twenty-six points. Larry Eustachy, coach of Colorado State, does a fantastic job with that program. He was also a good prognosticator. Tom Jurich, our athletic director at Louisville, was a college roommate and old friend of Eustachy's. He said

Larry came up to him after his press conference, patted him on the back, and said, "Buckle up."

It was going to be some kind of ride. We left Lexington headed for the Sweet Sixteen with more pressure headed our way. But it was just great to have our ally grow larger. Our next opponent, Oregon, was a No. 12 seed, but I expected that team to test us in every way, from our press to our athleticism and depth. The Ducks would be able to match it all. Their guards were lightning-quick and gave us all we could handle. They were extremely well coached and ready for our defense. Frankly, we probably wouldn't have won that game if we hadn't had a player off the bench turn in the best game of his career—Kevin Ware. Kevin had been doing a great job defensively for us, but in this game they had no answer for his penetration to the basket. Kevin slashed for eleven points and they were all huge in a 77–69 win, our first single-digit win in nearly a month. All week, our team had been sick. We hacked and coughed our way through practices and the shootaround, and the game was no different. Nobody was sicker than Russ Smith, but nobody was better. He finished with thirty-one points and we were, for a second straight year, on the doorstep of the Final Four.

The time had come to replace a great memory in Indianapolis. Twenty-one years ago I was part of arguably the greatest NCAA game ever played. My Kentucky team lost to Duke 104–103 in overtime in a regional final, after our best player, Jamal Mashburn, fouled out in regulation. I never talked about that game in negative terms. It was an awesome display of offense by both teams. Duke went on to win a well-deserved national championship and the game itself has become more iconic with every passing year.

Before the game, I did something I do not usually do. I brought up the past. For the first time, I would return to that Duke-UK game in a pregame speech. I told our guys that the stakes were the same as twenty-one years ago, a bid to the Final Four, but that this time the Blue Devils would not be victorious. We had lost to Duke in the Bahamas back in November. We had been without Gorgui Dieng in that five-point loss, and after that game I had told our guys, "We're going to see them again, and we will have Gorgui, and we will beat them." I had been right about the first two things. Now we would see if I had been right about the outcome.

So much of what people remember of that game surrounds Kevin Ware's injury that it might be one of our more overlooked performances of the season. We struggled in the aftermath of Kevin going down. Most of us don't remember the final minutes of the first half. Our guys were in shock and I didn't want them sitting around too much at halftime just thinking about it. We had played great basketball. From an assignment standpoint, we were truly on our game. I just told the guys, if we couldn't get Kevin back home to Atlanta for the Final Four, then the season wouldn't have been worth playing. There wasn't much else to say.

The game was a dogfight at the first media timeout of the second half. We were tied at 42, and honestly, the scenario didn't look good. Peyton Siva, Gorgui Dieng, and Wayne Blackshear all had three fouls. Our bench was shortened with the loss of Ware. Most teams in that situation, in a game of that magnitude, with that much pressure bearing down, would've wavered. Ours never did. We scored seven straight points, a Russ Smith drive and foul off a pick-and-roll, a jumper by Peyton, and a put-back by Chane. Coach Krzyzewski called timeout, but after having our balloon deflate, we were beginning to inflate again. After two Duke free throws, Peyton took over. He found Gorgui for a layup, then got a defensive rebound and went coast-to-coast to put us up nine. Duke never got any closer the rest of the game. In all, it was a 20–4 run, in what wound up being a twenty-two-point victory. It was the epitome of a team effort. Coach K was his usual class man in defeat. It's a shame more coaches who brush by the victorious coach with a dead-fish handshake would not take note of Coach K and learn how to act in victory as well as defeat.

"I thought we had a chance there, and then boom,"

Krzyzewski said. "And that's what they do to teams. They can boom you. They, whatever, my vocabulary isn't very good, but I hope you understand what I mean. It's a positive thing for them. Not for us. . . . They were terrific today. We would have to play great to beat them today, and we were playing pretty well. And then, boom, there's that. Now I'm going to say that for the rest of my life." He's not the only one. We're going to be saying it around the University of Louisville for a while, too. After the championship, we printed up team posters with the words "Boom Boys" in large letters and Coach K's quote at the bottom.

After the game on CBS, commentator Seth Davis said this: "So much for there being no dominant team in college basketball. That was a dominant performance."

We were on our way to Atlanta, Kevin Ware's hometown. Kevin would be on the trip with us, along with our old travel partner riding in the front seat—pressure.

After watching ten game films on Wichita State, I knew this would be our toughest opponent of the season. The Shockers had a deep and talented team that was holding opponents to 39 percent shooting from the field. I reiterated to our team that this game would not resemble Oregon or Duke. This game would be won by the team that defended its goal with the most intensity. Wichita State did not let you enter the lane without five people in your lap. The only time we would be able to get into the paint would be after quick ball and player movement. It would be tough without a backcourt substitute. We would have to call on our walk-on, Tim Henderson, to give us quality minutes. The last time I had put Tim into a game he ran to the scorer's table and tripped and fell on his own towel. The game was the struggle we predicted. Points were difficult to come by against Wichita State's defense. You could sense the nervousness from the large contingent of Louisville fans. Down twelve points with thirteen minutes left in the game, Luke drove and passed to none other than Tim Henderson in the right corner. I yelled to Tim to kill it, and he did. Down nine we got another stop and Russ penetrated and hit Tim Henderson again in the right corner. This time I said nothing. I didn't want to push my luck. Tim let it go again and made it, and in doing that, changed the entire complexion of the game. In forty-two seconds, he had cut our deficit in half. As we look back, a little used walk-on saved the day and brought us to that one shining moment, the championship game.

Now pressure came to the forefront and loomed larger than ever. With an hour and a half devoted to the media on the Sunday before the game, the question was asked a dozen times: Would the season be a failure if we didn't win the championship? Now, I've given the speech before about standing on the podium with silver medals around our necks after four years of hard work for our seniors. This Olympics comparison worked well for a team that was proud but having to settle for second place as someone else's national anthem was being played. But the media was right. I'm not sure if we would have viewed the season as a failure if we had lost in the championship game, but the all-out pressure we faced going into it was of that magnitude, and we were ready to face it.

Michigan was another extremely well-coached team, and maybe as good a shooting team as I've seen. But I didn't expect Spike Albrecht, a backcourt substitute averaging 1.7 points per game, to go for seventeen in the first half. I asked Russ Smith, who was telling his teammates before the game he was anxious to guard player of the year Trey Burke, if he minded forgetting about Trey and trying to guard a guy who was averaging less than two points a game. Down twelve once again, it was Luke Hancock time. With four straight threes from Luke, we charged back to take the lead briefly before trailing by only two at halftime. In the locker room, I told them I did not want to see Albrecht score again. We also talked about getting their bigs into difficult situations guarding pick-and-rolls. We would have our power forward, Chane Behanan, roam the baseline looking for rebounds and feeds for dunks.

Chane played his best game of the season. Gorgui played his best game of the season. Luke played his best game of the season. And Peyton played his best game of the season. And we needed every bit of it in a championship game for the ages, an 82–76 win that culminated in a Louisville celebration. Twenty-seven years had passed without Louisville winning a championship, and there were so many heroes in a beautifully played final game by both teams. College basketball needed a great championship game, and got it in a big way. Pressure had carried our team to excellence. And with the ghosts of the Duke game slimed forever, it was time for me to reflect.

Our championship is shared with every Louisville fan, in a city that totally knows how to celebrate. At some point, I was asked about one of my favorite moments. It was an easy answer.

After walking in to check on Kevin Ware at the hospital in Indianapolis, the surgeons met me in the lobby. They told me the surgery went well and he would make a full recovery in time. The next week would be important to make sure there was no infection from the bone having been exposed, but they were confident he was going to be all right. That's all I needed to hear. As I look back as a teacher of basketball and life lessons to young athletes, the whole moment summed up much of what I strive for. You had genuine emotions on the part of players for each other. You had courage displayed by Kevin in telling his teammates to just win the game, and by the rest of our guys for overcoming their emotions and going out and getting the job done. You would've thought, after all those years since the greatest college game ever played, I would cherish a twenty-two-point victory like few others in my career. Instead, I cherish that moment, seeing those young men react to such a difficult situation with courage and character.

If there is pressure in your own life, don't fight it. Let it be a force that propels you to a greater performance. Just recently I watched Carmelo Anthony of the New York Knicks in a press conference after a victory. He told the media that he doesn't want pressure, but rather feels that enjoying the moment will be easier. He doesn't realize the significance of pressure. He's a great talent and when he embraces the pressure that comes with his talent he'll become a better player with a better understanding of why he succeeds. I think about his statement, then about Michael Jordan, who put that pressure upon himself to be the greatest player in every game. That was his driving force. Melo needs to look at pressure as that driving influence.

Pressure should not be your enemy. Learn from it. Prepare, practice, and be ready to perform under the influence of pressure. It's what drives you toward excellence. With the majority of our team back from a championship season, pressure will be there waiting for us when we return to practice in the fall. And we will be glad to greet it as an old friend.

10

Building Your Bridge

When I first got into coaching at the age of twenty-four at Boston University, my thoughts and aspirations were of winning basketball games, developing great players, designing great offenses and defenses, and climbing the ladder of success. As I have crossed the threshold of age sixty, however, I'm no longer thinking about that ladder. Now I think more about a bridge. That's the imagery that has been in my mind lately as I look back on my career and realize that just as much as the victories, it's the people you worked with and walked with across the bridge to their own success that mean more than anything. Certainly, any schoolteacher or manager understands this imagery. It's the essence of what being a leader is all about, and I feel fortunate as I look back to see a crowded bridge. I got into coaching to win games and because of my love for the game. Part of working with players, however, is helping them cross that bridge from being college students to successful young people. What I never expected when I launched into coaching was looking around at my bridge at this point in my career and seeing so many other coaches having crossed it along with me. I did not set out to be a trainer of coaches, it just seemed to happen as a by-product of the way we did things, and of my great joy in seeing people who have worked for us go on to be successful on their own. I've always felt that lending a hand to help people reach their potential is what leadership is all about. When I'm asked how it has happened that twenty-eight coaches, players, or managers have come from my teams to land head coaching jobs of their own, there is no single answer. Certainly, I look for future head coaches when I am looking for assistants. I want someone with ambition and hunger. Still, I have hired guys who I had little idea would make it big in the profession, only to see them do just that.

One major key is that you never judge by first impressions or secondhand reports. The adage says you can't judge a book by its cover. That is right. I've had so many illustrations of people making it big in our industry that you never would have identified with such ability or potential at first glance. You never truly know what's the inner drive of a person. I remember a handwritten letter by a young man from New Jersey who wanted to learn our system and serve as a student manager. I was the head coach at Kentucky and returned his letter suggesting he would be better served to apply at schools in New Jersey. I informed him that UK was predominantly Kentuckians and he might feel like a duck out of water. I suggested that he look at Seton Hall or some of the other programs in the Northeast. He was not deterred and wrote back that he wanted to study our style of play. I agreed and Frank Vogel was hired as one of ten people who would aid our team on the periphery. Like most student managers, he worked diligently to do all the grunt work with very little recognition, only earning increased financial aid with more time served in the program. This young man was a true student of the game, a good high school player who wanted to learn all facets of our profession. After graduation he became a graduate assistant helping with our video and scouting operation. When I moved on to become coach of the Boston Celtics, he came along as video coordinator. After my departure, he stayed on and helped my assistant Jim O'Brien when he took over as head coach of the Celtics. Of course, today Frank is the highly successful coach of the Indiana Pacers. Frank had energy and drive. His strong ambition helped him achieve a level of success that I never could have imagined when I was reading that initial letter. Through hard work, and given just a crack at an opportunity, he crossed that bridge with so many of the managers and assistant coaches I've had whose dream was to learn and one day run their own program.

Sometimes you know when people are going to be successful. I never had any doubt about Billy Donovan, though I always encouraged him to go into business or something that might make more money than coaching. He was another who would not be deterred, and sitting in the stands watching him win the national championship with Florida was one of my proudest moments.

More often, however, you reach out to assistants because something in them strikes you as promising, even if you're not sure how they will pan out. Marvin Menzies started out running nightclubs and bakery shops— hardly the typical coaching background. But I had learned by that time to be open to any kind of experience, as long as the person appeared passionate and knowledgeable. As it turned out, Marvin was a bundle of energy and he and his wife, Tammy, were a fantastic duo in making our program successful. Marvin now is head coach at New Mexico State, and I heard from him during our tournament run. One afternoon a gift came to the hotel. I opened it and it was a huge framed coaching tree, with small photos of everyone who has ever coached for me and gone on to become a head coach, signed and placed over a beautifully drawn tree. Looking at it, I can't help but be struck at how fortunate I've been to work with so many talented people.

I will admit I wasn't sure about one young assistant I brought on at Providence. He had limited experience playing the game, didn't play in college, and I wasn't sure he had the stature to climb to great heights in our game. But after watching his tremendous dedication and overwhelming love for the game, including sleeping nights in the coaches' office so he would be the first one in, I knew Jeff Van Gundy could accomplish anything he wanted in this business. And he has, both as a successful NBA coach and a fantastic analyst.

I never thought a guy like Reggie Theus, who had been an NBA All-Star and a legitimate TV and movie star, would be the kind of person who would make the kinds of sacrifices that a coach in our system has to make. Again, it was an assumption that was incorrect. Reggie's problem was that everyone else thought the way I had thought. But when I talked to Reggie and realized that this big-time NBA veteran had coached for a year as a volunteer assistant at Cal State–Los Angeles, I realized he was a guy who was willing to pay the price. He was a fantastic assistant, a great recruiter, and in his short time in Louisville helped us guide the program back to its first Final Four since 1986. He was a serious basketball guy who just needed someone to take his coaching ambitions seriously.

Some coaches and leaders, I've noticed over the years, want to be the smartest guy in the room. That's an attitude to be avoided. I was looking for assistants who would take ownership in the program, who would be serious every day about challenging all in our program to be their best while also showing a work ethic that was second to none. I understand now better than I ever have, if I can find someone with that incredible drive but also incredible humility, I know I've found someone who not only is going to do a great job for us, but someone who is going to be successful over the long haul.

That humility is a common denominator in those who have passed through my staff to go onto long and successful coaching careers. Whether you're talking about Billy Donovan, Tubby Smith, Frank Vogel, or others, it not only sets up an attitude of improvement, focus, and positive work ethic, but it enables them to withstand the rigors of the profession on their own.

I get so many calls, texts, and notes from former assistants now in the coaching ranks, and they are always grateful. But here's something I realized. Seeing them all do so well has played a significant part in my longevity and effectiveness as a coach. I've learned something from all of them. But it's more than that. I first experienced this when I was coach at Boston University, when I watched my good friend and former assistant Bill Burke move on to become head coach at Loyola of Baltimore. Keeping up with Bill and watching him build a program there gave me as much excitement, energy, and esteem as any victory. When it happened again with other former players or assistants, I noticed the same thing.

Our guys work long and hard. Long before the NCAA's twenty-hour working day maximum rule was mandated, our coaches came in at 5:45 A.M. and worked all day, until our three-on-three coaches' game ended in the evening. Our players were putting in a session before breakfast, had between-class shooting, and individual instruction before finally getting down to a team practice. I was, in those early days, only a few years older than my junior and senior players. The more I watched them achieve, the higher my self-esteem would rise, and the more motivated I would be. I didn't realize it back then, but I was building a bridge that so many others would cross. Individual honors are nice. But when one of your coaches or players moves up that ladder of success, you put your head on your pillow and smile with a great sense of pride and happiness for them.

Boston University was my first laboratory to tinker with a running, pressing system. I look back to my team picture there, and between players and coaches, three went to the NBA, one as a head coach, another a chief scout for the Celtics, and a third assisting Greg Popovich with the San Antonio Spurs. Three others became college head coaches. At Providence College, I witnessed some of the lowest esteem I've ever encountered when first getting together with the players. They were a perennial doormat in the Big East, but behind an unbelievable work ethic, led by Billy the Kid Donovan, in our second season that team went to the Final Four. We celebrated together when Billy won back-to-back national titles as a coach. And in April of 2012, we celebrated our twenty-fifth anniversary of that Final Four run. It was great to see these men, and to experience a bond that lasts a lifetime. Dave Kipfer, our power forward who made us tougher in practice each day, told me then that he'd been sober for three years. I told him what he was accomplishing was as great as any Final Four. The esteem I saw those guys build at Providence came back to me in self-confidence and energy. Your esteem is your true self-worth. And when you help someone cross that bridge, your self-worth increases. I was a wealthy man at a very young age without ever realizing it. Ever since then, at every stop, the bridge has been building, with a steady stream of traffic crossing from training to sustained success. Looking back on those stops, I count it a rich experience.

Some of the wealthiest people in America are not listed in *Forbes* magazine. They are teachers, hospice workers, and many others working for religious and charitable organizations. Their bank accounts won't reflect much monetary evidence, but what they have in terms of true worth and happiness cannot be matched or bought. What good is a long career, even a successful one, if you reach the end of your bridge and look around only to find yourself alone, or to regret not bringing more people along on your journey or helping them start theirs?

We've talked a great deal in this book about weathering difficult times. A time comes—and the last pages of this book provide the perfect time to discuss this—when your focus has to be on more than just getting yourself up the ladder or through the storm. At some point, you need to consider whether you are helping others across the bridge or through their own hard times. Extending a hand to others is more than a Good Samaritan cliché. There is reward for the giver, as well. An outward focus always leads to inward renewal.

Not everyone will find sustained success. Like most of us, some who have been on the bridge with you will encounter difficult times. This is where loyalty is required. There can be no toll on your bridge. You cannot exact a cost. And it must always remain open. Antoine Walker was a brash college athlete who helped us win a championship at Kentucky. He became a top-five draft choice of the Boston Celtics. I later coached him with that storied franchise, as well. Upon my return to college basketball, I became uneasy listening to all the stories about his gambling and lifestyle. It was a tragic story, one of $120 million squandered, though the story is not unique to Antoine.

"The lifestyle I set up for myself at age nineteen was the start of the problem," he told Ricki Lake on her talk show in early 2013. "I set up my family in a certain lifestyle. I had a lot of friends. I traveled with seven or eight guys, and I wanted to help them. I was young and energetic. I wasn't thinking about being smart with money at that time."

Although our relationship was not as good when with the Celtics as it was at Kentucky, today the bridge must stay open to all. I'm trying to help Antoine both spiritually as well as in other areas. All stories can't end with some magical path to success. We must never turn our back on those who helped us in life. Antoine helped me to a lifetime goal. I need to be there for him. I know firsthand that there will be many needing a hand to help cross that bridge. I have vowed to help all those willing to help themselves. Gifts are to be given without keeping score or wanting recognition. They are the most cherished things we have in our lives. The more people we can help cross that bridge, the more we understand the true meaning of building it.

One main facet of lending that hand to cross the bridge is forgiveness. In my early years, I would dismiss any athlete who didn't return the loyalty shown to them. That was a shortcoming on my part. I didn't understand the tremendous power of forgiveness. Today I'm armed with both the wisdom that allows me to see beyond those that travel a one-way street, and the experience to know that we all come up short at times. We all cross together as one regardless of our shortcomings. It's when people are in need that we should look to come alongside them, not go the other way. I've told Antoine, I can't fathom how a player could squander that amount of money. But loyalty transcends such things. When I heard Antoine say he would make his millions back in a syndicated TV show, I cringed at that statement. My hope is that he will get involved helping athletes avoid making the same mistakes he made, and help them cross that bridge to true prosperity. If he can do that, he will begin to capture so much more than the millions he hopes to regain. Building a bridge is about creating hope from despair, creating a road that will lead to true happiness.

One of my favorite instances of this came with a young man who had come to Louisville from Nigeria, Muhammed Lasege. His story was remarkable. He was so eager to find opportunity in this nation to play basketball that he signed on with some outfit in Russia that claimed to find foreign players spots at American universities, but instead mainly got those kids into Russia and took advantage of them, having them play on their club teams and intimidating them into doing what they wanted them to do. Somehow, Muhammed managed to get to this country and finally landed a spot at Louisville, before my arrival there. The NCAA, however, had other ideas. First it questioned his academics, but when he had nearly straight As during his first year at Louisville while he waited to be cleared to play, those questions were put to rest. Next, the NCAA said he broke rules by accepting improper benefits on his way to the United States. Now, Muhammed had never seen an NCAA rulebook, but by signing what he thought was a work agreement with the Russian club, he had, by the NCAA's definition, signed a contract with an agent, and therefore was ruled permanently ineligible. Muahmmed sued and won the right to play for a time, but in the end the Kentucky Supreme Court sided with the NCAA, and his college career was over. I was his coach when that happened and I was astounded that the NCAA was not going to let a model student play basketball. I'm still disappointed by it. They said he had an "intent to professionalize." No, his true intent was to play college basketball and receive an education in the United States.

But even after he could not play for our team, he remained one of our family. I was able, along with others in Louisville, to help him finish his education. He got a job working for Humana in Louisville. But when the U.S. cut the number of work visas issued one year, Muhammed learned that he was going to have to leave the country. At that point, I realized he needed help if he was going to continue his journey across that bridge, even after so promising a start. I told Muhammed it was time to put his basketball skills to work, and he did. He played in various countries, some in Europe, and made good money playing pro basketball in Iran. What was his goal? Not to play professional basketball, but to save up enough money so that when he returned to the United States, he could attend graduate school.

That's just what he did. He came back to this country and was accepted into the prestigious Wharton School of Business at the University of Pennsylvania. The Ivy League admissions boards were impressed with how he had handled all the adversity sent his way by the NCAA, and were impressed with his willingness to do whatever it took to reach his goals. With that master's degree in hand, Muhammed went to work as an executive for Exxon, and he remains there today with his wife and children in Houston, Texas. With his background in accounting, business, oil, and international finance, along with a humble, persevering spirit, he is well positioned for a lifetime of success. Even when the bridge appeared closed to him, it was important to me to help him find a way across, and he certainly displayed the character to remove the obstacle that was set before him, eventually turning it to his favor.

My bridge is crowded right now, with guys who have come through our program as players or coaches and learned lessons that have brought them success and, more importantly, happiness, over the years. In turn, many of them have brought many others across the bridge with them. Their success is their own. I was just a playmaker, handing out assists to help people reach their potential. But in the end, I'm not sure anything in life can give you more joy or satisfaction than helping people cross that bridge. This is the true end of all your efforts and striving. Right now in my office, I look at the NCAA championship trophy, sitting amid a pile of mail that has been sent to me by people, and feel great pride in our players and great memories of what we did. In the background, I look at all those smiling faces of coaches in the frame that Marvin Menzies sent me, and I feel satisfaction and contentment. The bridge is crowded, and it is good. When I finally retire someday, my life will be full rooting for all those people who helped me build my bridge, and I sincerely thank all of those who allowed me to cross with them.

It did not begin with me. As a sophomore in high school, I remember going to the Five-Star basketball camp. The camp only lasted one week, but it was like going to Carnegie Hall. I sat there as a camper and just reveled in the things these coaches were saying. It was like going to a concert and finding out what bands you liked the most. I was mesmerized by these coaches, but by four in particular. I was in awe of Hubie Brown's strength of voice in commanding attention and covering every detail as if the world hinged on it. I was captivated by Dick Vitale's passion and enthusiasm, and how he talked about his life. Bob Knight struck fear in every camper as he spoke. You were in fear that a basketball would come flying at your head if you dared let your eyes wander to something else—because it would. Chuck Daly came across as if he was a CEO, someone who had every hair in place and in total command of what he was talking about and what he was doing.

Today, I can see the influence of each of those men as my career unfolded. They were not yet giants in the profession. Only Knight was nationally known. But to me, they were rock stars. I took so much from Hubie Brown, from his preparation and attention to detail right down to his expressions. I took some of Dick Vitale's passion and undying love of the game. I learned the importance of commanding the respect and attention of your players from Bob Knight. And I wanted to make the kind of impression that I had seen Chuck Daly make. When I took over at Boston University, all of those things were in my mind. To be voted into the Hall of Fame, where each of those men wait, is more than a little surreal to me. I made it across that bridge. I thank God that so many stand with me as I cross.

I've been lucky in my thirty-five years of coaching. The more I reach out to people, the more rewarding each day becomes. Loyalty does build trust and certainly forgiveness allows us to have a crowded bridge. I'm at peace today as a leader and it's a wonderful gift that's been given to me—a crowded bridge with so many stories of crossing. Nothing could be more rewarding. You can build that bridge for yourself, by learning from your mentors, and passing along your knowledge to those who are willing to cross that bridge with you.

EPILOGUE

Our NCAA championship experience ended with a trip to the White House, one that none of us ever will forget. Leaving the White House, I thought about all that had transpired, all our players had overcome, and I was so happy for all of them. President Obama mentioned so many by name in his outstanding speech. He noted Luke Hancock's Most Outstanding Player accomplishment and Peyton Siva's contributions, even talked about how excited they were about Gorgui Dieng in his native Senegal. He not only mentioned Russ Smith, who wasn't at the White House visit because he was playing basketball in Estonia, but mentioned the nickname "Russdiculous," which all our guys loved. He talked about Kevin Ware's courage. And the very first player he mentioned was Tim Henderson. Think about it—the leader of the free world, mentioning a walk-on from Christian Academy in Louisville. I could not have been more proud.

"They didn't just show it on the court; they showed it in the classroom and in the community," the president said.

President Obama kidded me over the tattoo I got after we won the championship. I promised the players I would get one, and I had to follow through. He told me I had earned something that will live forever—"a shirtless picture of yourself on the Internet."

That isn't all that will endure. The lessons we learned along the way will stay with us, too. It was a wonderful way to cap off a season that we all will remember, a season that has left its mark on all of us.

There is not a doubt in my mind that the one-day contract I committed to played a major role in our success. It made our focus sharp, and regardless of deficit our guys never panicked. We utilized technology the correct way, to help us meticulously prepare. Our distractions were kept to a minimum with our eyes remaining on the cutting down of the net after the championship game, but not until then. And I am confident we will hold onto our Ph.D.—being passionate, hungry and driven—into next season. How could we not? We all signed a one-day contract.

ACKNOWLEDGMENTS

A book, like a championship basketball season, does not happen by accident. But I find that the people who helped me the most with this book have been people who helped me in life. All of the athletes and assistant coaches who helped me build a bridge for all of us to cross provide me with continual joy and satisfaction.

Tom Jurich, vice president for athletics at the University of Louisville, afforded me all the tools it took to return the basketball program here to the success it so richly deserved. Beyond that, he has been my close friend and professional confidant, and himself has become a historic figure at the university.

Not enough is said about Kenny Klein. As sports information director, he is the best in the country, but he's more than that. Kenny sets a standard for professionalism that anyone who has worked with him will tell you is second to none. More than that, he is my close friend.

Thanks also to Jordan Sucher, my executive assistant, Vinny Tatum, our equipment manager, Stephanie Davis, basketball receptionist. These are people who keep our office running—and in the case of Vinny, laughing.

And finally thanks to two men who don't get enough credit in our program's success. Fred Hina, our trainer, is the best in the game. After years with the New York Mets, he has served us well. Ray Ganong, our strength and conditioning coach, keeps us running, and running, and running. Thanks to all.